Dedication

To our two beautiful children, Hope Cherish ...

This book is about a journey, one which you are just beginning, the journey of discovering who you truly are.

I pray that you will both discover the journey God has predestined for your life. That you will love your journey; fill it with fun, adventure, wisdom, laughter and great travelling companions. I pray that you will journey in strength and grace, and show compassion and kindness to all those who you encounter along the way. Most of all I pray that you will make your journey your own and be your gorgeous selves.

I will always be your greatest cheerleader and friend. I love you more than I could ever express.

Love from

Mum

Contents

‘ To be **nobody-but-yourself**

in a world
which is doing its best,
night and day,

to make **you**
everybody else -

means to **fight**
the hardest battle
which any
human being can fight;
and **never**
stop fighting. ’

E E Cummings

Let the Journey Begin

This book is about a journey; one that I believe we all must embark upon. It's a journey that some people may never take, or even be aware of. For others, it's a journey that they feel is too personal to talk about. It is the journey of discovering who you really are.

This journey confronts you with the question, 'Who am I?' and demands that you move beyond answering it with any title, label or role that you currently fulfil in life. If your answer to this question would be couched in the terms of a clinical job description, or an explanation of what you currently do in life, then this is a tell-tale sign that, maybe for you, the journey has not yet begun.

This journey challenges you to think about what makes you unique; and makes you think about what God has placed in your life that sets you apart from everyone else. It will cause you to examine what makes you stand out from the crowd and makes you different. This journey opens your eyes to a whole world of possibilities that you may never have realised existed. It's not necessarily an easy journey to take, because what you discover may make demands on you that are hard to follow through. It may call for you to make some changes to things like your career, relationships and, in general, could re-route your life. We only have one life, and I am more aware than ever that this is our one chance to make our own unique mark. I, for one, want to make sure that the route I take in life is the most fulfilling and liberating life possible; that my journey gets everything out of me God intended, and that I get everything out of the journey God has in it for me.

When you were young, did you ever learn to ride a bicycle with the help of stabilisers, or training wheels, as they are sometimes called? If so, you will understand that they had the capacity to fool you into thinking that you could ride confidently and had mastered the skill of bicycle riding, only to discover later that you hadn't! All along you had been protected and stabilised by the training wheels, but one day the stabilisers were taken off, and as you began to wobble, fall off, graze your leg, get back on and wobble some more, you realised that the hard work of learning to ride by yourself had only just begun, because the support that had kept you upright was gone. This is what it's like when we set off on the journey to discover who we really are.

At thirty-three years of age I am on that journey. I thought I knew who I was, but over the past few years I began to realise, that in some areas, I still had my stabilisers on. I hadn't even begun to try and let the real me come to the surface and remove the support I was so heavily resting upon. I had to face the fact that, if I started to remove some of my stabilisers, I would have to risk people seeing the real me. Inside myself I had a battle going on. I knew it was the right thing to do but I didn't want other people to see me wobble and take a tumble; I didn't want them to see me careering along feeling out of control. I thought I was a confident rider, yet my confidence in some areas was in the training wheels, and if I was to continue with my journey I had to let them go.

I now realise that this journey of identity is a life-long one which I must thoroughly explore if I am to discover who I am. This has meant that in areas of my life I have had to detach from people, comforts, and securities that were acting as my spiritual stabilisers. Since then I have fallen off my 'bike' a few times, I have grazed my knee and made mistakes along the way, but now I can confidently say I have found my balance and am learning how to ride in my own right. The first time you set off without the familiar training wheels, it can be daunting, and you can end up worrying about the wobbles that lie ahead, but once you realise they are part of what God intends you to go through, instead of fearing them, you can begin to embrace them. Now when I see people who appear to be confidently coasting through life, I am not intimidated by their apparent skill and how easy they make it look. Instead, I have a good look to see whether their stabilisers are still on! I have been surprised how many seemingly confident riders are actually not riding on their own yet. This should be an encouragement to us all — we are not alone!

In this book, I want to share with you some of my journey, some of the 'stabilisers' I have had to remove and some of the bumps and grazes I have collected along the way. You have incredible potential in your life, but the only way to maximise it is to commit to this journey of becoming the person God created you to be. I want to invite you to walk with me for a while as we look at this identity journey. It is a journey of both separation and connection. It brings separation from any labels you have carried that don't fit the real you, and connection to the relationships God has for your life. I have discovered this journey brings with it change, challenge, disorientation and moments of sheer panic, but the benefits far outweigh the cost.

So, wherever you are at, whether you have already started your journey of identity, or whether you were never aware of it before, I want to challenge you to look intently at your life and be willing to ask the question, 'Who am I?'

Chapter 1

100 Percent You

Jesus was given many labels and badges in his lifetime, but he refused to wear any of them. He was difficult to define because there had never been anyone like him before. None of the usual labels fitted; he wasn't a religious person, he wasn't a politician and he wasn't someone who fitted into the mould of scholar. He wasn't a highly-educated, well-known leader and he didn't come from the kind of place that people thought a world changer should come from. He was just a boy growing up in a very ordinary home, in a very ordinary town, learning the very ordinary trade of carpentry from his father, Joseph.

None of this mattered to Jesus. He wasn't flustered or upset that people couldn't work out how to describe him. He wasn't bothered when he was wrongly labelled, because labels, badges and roles meant nothing to him. Why? Because when you are one hundred percent confident in who you are as a person, you need nothing else to define you. Jesus didn't come to be defined, he arrived knowing who he was and where he was journeying to, so he was totally himself. They would eventually have to create a new vocabulary to describe him.

You could tell Jesus was one hundred percent himself because he didn't conform to any mould placed upon him. He would embrace children one day and hold the attention of vast crowds the next. He expressed his heart and was not afraid to hold back his passions; from showing his grief over Lazarus to his extreme anger with the money-changers in the temple, from his clear disgust of the religious hypocrites to strongly confronting, even potentially offending those closest to him.

Jesus was different things to different people. To some he was a man of compassion, to some a friend, to some a healer, to some a great teacher and to others an inspirational leader. What impacted people about him wasn't something they could describe by giving him a badge, it was his personhood. Every person whose life was touched by him, found him forever memorable. Jesus knew people struggled to see where he fitted and even asked his disciples who they thought he was. We read in Matthew that,

'When Jesus came to the region of Caesarea Philippi, he asked his disciples, "Who do people say the son of man is?" They replied, "Some say John the Baptist, others say Elijah, and still others say Jeremiah or one of the prophets." "But what about you?" he asked. "Who do you say I am?"

Simon Peter answered, "You are the Christ, the son of the living God."' (Matthew 16:13-16)

When Jesus heard their answer, he didn't rush out to correct people who said he was John the Baptist or Jeremiah and explain they were mistaken. It didn't matter to him what the religious leaders or the crowds thought of him. Those who were closest to him, those who were on the journey with him, understood that none of those titles fitted because they knew the real Jesus.

Jesus gave us a blueprint for how he wanted us to live life. He modelled what it means to live being one hundred percent yourself; being totally liberated and free to express yourself in a way that glorifies God but without holding any of your true self back. He showed what understanding your true identity looks like. A look at the complete liberty and ease he had with who he was, shows how far we all have to go on our own journeys. It also explains how Jesus got so much done in his three years of ministry. He wasn't held back by people, feelings, or approvals. He didn't spend hours wasting time in meetings he didn't need to be in. He wasn't constrained by agendas, muzzled by peer pressure, or confined by the status quo. He had no 'stabilisers', but had a perfectly balanced life because he was one hundred percent himself.

We have access to the same liberty and freedom that Jesus expressed. Therefore, the House of God should be the first place anyone should go to see what 'one hundred percent living' looks like. So much about our lives, the way he made us as individuals, the amazing difference and diversity in creation, points to the fact that we were designed with this kind of living in mind; an existence where we can all enjoy being the unique individuals he has created us to be.

Sadly, it can be hard to find churches and Christians who are expressing their lives and the life of Christ to the full one hundred percent. So many Christians are not one hundred percent about anything, especially their identity, because many are not one hundred percent sure of their own identity in him. I have had too many experiences of meeting Christians and walking into churches where everybody just seems the same. People dress the same, act the same and speak the same and it's so boring! They have taken Christianity and prescribed to people what it should look like. They have tried to tell people who and what they should be. Instead of the church being a place that people can go to and find the most diverse mix of people imaginable – a rich tapestry with every colour, race, hairstyle, shape and size celebrating who they are in God's House – it has become a place where people look like they have come off a production line! Church has been turned into a 'one size and style fits all' experience.

So, let me ask you a question about your life? Are you one hundred percent 'you' like Jesus was? There is no-one on this planet who is just like you or just like me. You have an individual thumb-print; the iris in your eye is different to everyone else's and you have a unique DNA code. I am sure it would have been far easier for God to set up a people-production line and make everyone the same, but that was never his plan. This in itself shows that God made you as an original. The question is, are you expressing that originality through your life? Jesus set us an amazing example of what one hundred percent living looks like, and we need to aim for that kind of living if we want our lives to make an impact on the world in the time we have left.

Celebrate or tolerate

One of the things we have fought for, in our journey as a church, is the empowerment of people to be themselves and to live out all that God intended them to be. This sounds like a great value to have. However, it is a value many want in theory but in practice feel it is too risky to endorse. That's because empowerment means you can't just theorise but must actively facilitate the diversity this brings; you have to encourage, embrace and celebrate difference. In our church, there was a time when you could predict what people would say, what they would wear and where they would sit in the services, but not anymore. We have been on a journey to find our identity as a church and this has taught us to celebrate difference, rather than tolerate it. We have learned to embrace all kinds of people and encourage everyone to be themselves, just as Christ modelled.

Recently, as I was in church worshipping God, I was filled with awe as I thought about all the amazing things he has done in the lives of so many of our church family. As I looked across the auditorium, I saw one of our most recent converts at the age of one hundred, worshipping alongside some of our youngest church members. As I looked at the stage, I suddenly saw it as a celebration of great difference. I saw unity amongst a great diversity of people and styles.

I looked at Mike Harvie, who is one of our awesome worship leaders — a young guy with a huge heart for God. Mike was lost in worship; jumping, singing and just being himself. Yet, I don't think Mike would find an easy 'fit' in many churches and I certainly can't think of many platforms where Mike would be celebrated. His two-tone hair, which is half long and half short, would put most people off, or certainly his lip ring may offend. Neither would his edgy dress-sense fit in. And, if all that was OK, I'm not sure they would appreciate the fact that Mike is our screaming worship leader! He has a unique scream that he uses to great effect in some of our songs. It is part of his personal musical style that, instead of controlling, we have empowered and made room for. What I love most about Mike is that all that he does comes from complete devotion to God and a sold-out heart for his House. He has written some of the loudest songs and the most devotional songs for our church. What can I say about him, except Mike is Mike! He is totally comfortable in being who God has called him to be and is a very colourful part of our team.

This is what I celebrate about the House of God; it is a place of such vibrant variety. We need more Houses that allow people to be themselves, otherwise many who have the potential to be awesome, dedicated followers of Christ will never find a place to call home; a place that encourages them to be one hundred percent themselves. Let me ask you a question. Do you go to church one hundred percent 'you'? Or are you hiding the real you and only showing people in your church the fifty per cent of yourself that you feel will be the most acceptable? Are there other sides of you that never come out in God's House because you just can't see where they would fit? Is there hidden creativity, gifting, talent, a dream or desire that you have silenced to ensure you don't upset the status quo? Of all places, God's House is where you can be one hundred percent 'you'; something which starts at the top, with senior leaders truly being themselves and creating a culture of acceptance and empowerment. As a result, the church becomes a place where 'stabilisers' are removed and people are constantly being liberated on their journey. It should never be a place where you come and find your life is 'wheel clamped'!

Colouring the elephant

Having so much variety under the same roof can be a very scary thought for some people and we are often asked how this mix of people can possibly fit and work together. When I'm training staff and helping them understand how our church works, I use the analogy of an elephant as an illustration. I explain that as a leadership, we have determined the shape of our House and established our vision, so we know we are building an 'elephant'. But this is just the outline and people are encouraged to be creative in bringing it to life. The team gets to choose how they colour it in and they can make it pink, blue, spotty or striped; we don't mind. We just want to get out the colours that are in their lives.

The shape of our vision is so clear that no-one entering our House could get the wrong idea. If someone decides they'd prefer it to be shaped like a giraffe, instead of an elephant, they will soon find out that isn't up for negotiation. Yet, within our chosen shape and vision, there is so much space created for people to express who they are and what God has called them to do as they colour it in.

Churches often make the mistake of spending more time and effort making sure that people know what they shouldn't be doing and what isn't allowed. This shuts people down, rather than opening them up to what is possible. Adam and Eve made a similar mistake in the

Garden of Eden; they had so much that was permissible for them to do and enjoy but ended up focusing on the one tree they were told not to touch.

In our churches we need to keep on celebrating all the space we are creating for people to be themselves. In my home church, we now have over one hundred and seventy ministries that people can get involved in. This says to them, find a place where you can best be yourself, a place where your gifts and talents can come to the fore. If you are creative, join the creative arts ministries. If you want to work with the hurting, join one of the inner city outreach ministries. If you love to teach, the media, cooking, or whatever else, there's a place for you, so come and find your fit. And if none fit, we actively encourage people to create a new ministry to express who they are in Christ. This empowers people to plug in to serving God, in line with their passions and interests. By doing this we are setting the big picture of the vision but letting people bring their own unique style and creativity to it.

Doing this also allows people to be themselves by not hiding their journey, but using it to glorify God because it is part of who they are. Take for example our prison ministry, which has received a commendation from HM Prison Service. This ministry is led by a wonderful man called Peter Hopla, who himself spent a period of time in prison some years ago. That time could have been a part of his journey he wanted to hide, a time when he failed God, his family and friends. But, by refusing to do that, he has now found a place that helps him make his past pay! He now gets to give himself away and bring fresh hope to many other prisoners. His openness about his journey now encourages them to embark on their own journey with Christ.

I believe that God encourages this and it's what he wants in his House, yet many church leaders remove this liberty for fear of losing control. They don't just tell you that they are going to have an 'elephant', they also tell you the size, the colour and the shade in infinite detail. This leaves no room for manoeuvre and doesn't allow people to express their own individuality and be themselves. If your least favourite colour is grey and that is the colour prescribed, you will probably end up unfulfilled, as your love of colouring things bright purple will not be appreciated!

We need to build churches that are helping people be themselves and are not turning everyone into charismatic clones. God wants you to be one hundred percent you. He wants you to discover who you really are and for that to be expressed through your life.

The more I study God's Word and look at the lives of people I admire, like David, Solomon, Ruth and Moses, the more I realise that each of them had to travel an amazing individual journey to discover their true identity and then achieve all they did. They didn't wake up one morning to discover they were called to save a nation. It was a process they went through and they experienced moments where their identity was at crisis point. If you are going through something similar today you are in good company, so be encouraged.

The story of one such person is that of Jacob. His identity journey is an amazing story and I want us to spend some time taking a closer look at his life and unpacking it together. His journey provides us with some useful sign posts to point us in the right direction as we embark on our own journeys, the journey of discovering who you really are and then living as 'one hundred percent' you!

Chapter 2

Identity Crisis

Jacob knew what it was like to be 'labelled' by others. He spent years trying to live up to the expectations placed on his shoulders by other people and experienced the weight of being forced into a role that didn't fit him. Jacob was a twin and from the very start, he and his brother Esau were jostling for position, even while they were still in the womb. Although they were twins, they were completely different in every other way. We read:

'When the time came for her to give birth, there were twin boys in her womb. The first to come out was red, and his whole body was like a hairy garment; so they named him Esau. After this, his brother came out, with his hand grasping at Esau's heel; so he was named Jacob. Isaac was sixty years old when Rebekah gave birth to them. The boys grew up, and Esau became a skillful hunter, a man of the open country, while Jacob was a quiet man, staying among the tents. Isaac, who had a taste for wild game, loved Esau, but Rebekah loved Jacob.' (Genesis 25:24-28)

Here were two brothers who had distinctly different personalities, interests and looks. You could never mistake one for the other; the rugged looks of Esau, the hunter, compared to the smooth-faced features of Jacob, who liked to stay at home. Despite their obvious differences, there was someone in Jacob's world who didn't appreciate or value him for who he was, and instead, started to compare the two boys with each other. We read that *'Rebekah loved her son Jacob but Isaac his father loved Esau.'* Jacob was his mother's favourite and, because of that, she desperately wanted him to succeed in life. So she schemed, plotted and manipulated to make sure this happened. Rebekah spent her life trying to make Jacob into Esau, because she wanted him to have the blessing and birthright of the firstborn son. Consequently, he ended up spending the first part of his life growing up in his brother's shadow and was not allowed to be his true self.

Whose life are you living?

Jacob didn't live his own life — he lived the life of his mother's choosing. She tried to make him identical to his brother in every way. Rather than celebrating the difference of her two boys, she manipulated her youngest son to try and become like his brother. I have often wondered why Jacob went along with his mother's manipulation. Why didn't he stand up and challenge her? Why didn't he say what he really felt?

Yet Jacob was not a one-off, he is a picture of many people who have also let the 'Rebekahs' in their world steer and dictate to them where their lives should be heading.

I think it's important to stop and think about why Jacob was such an easy target to manipulate. What was it about his character that made him so easy for Rebekah to shape? Jacob's journey had been restricted by Rebekah from a young age, because she wanted him to emulate his older brother rather than develop his own identity. Jacob, therefore, lacked momentum in his own life and one of the keys to keeping momentum in your own world comes from your identity journey. The resultant lack of movement in his own journey meant that he did not have enough momentum to overcome her pushiness. I'm sure there must have been times when Jacob was fed up with being compared to his brother and felt like saying, 'Hey! Stop it. I'm Jacob. Can't you just love me for being me?' But he wasn't sure who the real Jacob was. He was confused about his identity and that made it easy for Rebekah to manipulate him.

If you aren't clear about the direction you need to travel in, then the same thing can happen to you. Other people will flag you down and board your life. They will start to suggest routes that they would enjoy and you end up becoming a taxi for them by taking them to the place of their choosing, while you get further and further away from fulfilling the dreams in your own heart. That's why knowing who you are is a gift you give yourself and others around you. If you can say, 'this is me' and 'this is where I am heading', then people can make up their own mind whether they want to come with you or not. You need to set your co-ordinates in life to create movement and momentum in the direction you want to go. Certain people won't board your life anymore, because they know the destination is no longer up for discussion.

Jacob lived the first part of his life feeling neither hot nor cold towards his future or his own identity. He was lukewarm. He didn't have an opinion. He didn't speak up. He didn't fight for what he believed was right. He was not in control of his identity or journey. Therefore, his life was constantly compromised and diluted; it was lukewarm living and this became very costly. Revelation 3:15-16 warns against becoming this kind of person. It says that God himself hates lukewarm living and will spit you out of his mouth if you live that way. He can't do anything with a lukewarm life, because it's not the life he intended for you. Lukewarm people are easy targets for the enemy and ineffective for the kingdom, because, like Jacob, they have no backbone or conviction about things in their lives. Therefore, they have no direction set for their journey. Lukewarm people are easy to sway; they are easy to persuade and so often just end up going along with what other people say. They have a chameleon-type identity, which blends into whatever the strongest, most persuasive factor is in their world at any given time.

When our family goes out to eat, we have to be really careful about having a passive attitude to what food we want to order. Why? Because my mum likes to try different dishes and is great at persuading others to try what she really wants to eat. If we aren't sure what we fancy on the menu, she will come up with some great suggestions and end up ordering for us. She might want to try three or four dishes, so she gets other people to order her choices and then suggests that we all share them. She is very convincing and we often can end up eating her choice of meal!

This is an amusing example but when it is transferred to important decisions and choices you need to make, it becomes far more serious.   How many people are effectively eating what other people have ordered for them, living the life that other people said they should live and are not enjoying the meal being served to them? The real 'them' has completely different tastes, which will never be fulfilled while they have a passive attitude towards their journey. If you have a tendency to be lukewarm and indecisive, like Jacob, then you need to turn up the spiritual temperature of your life and start finding out what the real you wants, before others start deciding for you.

Pleasing Rebekah

As much as we need to be aware that there may be a Jacob-style weakness in us, we also need to be aware if there is a Rebekah strength in our lives. I need to say here that Rebekah wasn't a bad person. She loved Jacob, and wanted what she thought was the best for him. I have met many people like her, who have a great heart but have approached situations and used their strength of character in the wrong way. Strong personality types need to ensure they aren't insensitive when they are dealing with the Jacobs in their world. It can be right to give advice to people but we need to make sure that everything we do has a God-centred agenda, not our own. I have witnessed people giving guidance, when other motives are in play and a line has been crossed between giving guidance and trying to control others. Are they trying to manipulate people, or allowing them to be one hundred percent themselves? When it's manipulation, people end up doing something they don't enjoy but they often go along with it because of their heart to please 'Rebekah'.

I have had a passion to be in ministry from an early age. I'm not lukewarm about this; I'm red hot towards it because I know it is something that God has placed in me. It's part of what makes 'me' who I am. Because of this, I have frequently been asked by pastors to spend time with their children, to help develop them for a move into ministry. Each time I have simply replied by saying that the 'wrong person' is asking. If their children really want to be in ministry, that is great, but it must come from who they are; it must come from their desire to learn and embrace a role in ministry, not from the momentum of the family they have been born into. Being a pastor's kid was one of the labels attached to me, but it never owned me or determined who I was. I can honestly say, I have never been pushed or cajoled into being in ministry by my family. I have simply been encouraged to live my life with everything God has placed in me. I entered ministry because I wanted to and I am still in ministry because I have a passion to build God's House. However, many pastors who speak to me about their children assume their children will also be in ministry and this is a dangerous assumption. It can often lead to disappointment for the parents and unfair pressure on the child to do something that is not what they want. Do I believe that if you are a pastor's kid you will end up pastoring? Absolutely not! However, if the desire and gift to do ministry is in you, then go for it. The last thing I want to see are more Rebekahs steering Jacobs because of the strength of their own personalities, which will only result in more people being fifty percent themselves and fifty percent what others want them to be.

Life is simply too short to spend years doing things you don't enjoy and not being yourself. Jacob wasted his 'growing up years' not being able to enjoy his relationship with Esau, because he was competing with him, nor with his parents, because he was under pressure and those years were lost forever. I have met people who are living a 'Jacob existence' and not being themselves. At one conference, I remember being in the back room with the other guest speaker, before the meeting started. She was ashen-white and awfully nervous at the thought of having to speak. She was a fluent speaker in a one-on-one conversation but came across as very awkward and uncomfortable whenever she was in the pulpit. As I tried to build up her confidence, I felt the Holy Spirit say to me, 'Ask her what she loves to do!' At this question, her whole demeanour changed. 'Not many people ask me that,' she said and her face began to light up with passion and excitement as she told me of her love of interior design. She talked enthusiastically about how she loved to look at fabric swatches, paint colours and design room layouts and how she would really love to go to night school and learn more about it. I encouraged her to 'Go for it', because she would obviously love to do it. It was in keeping with who she was. 'Oh no,' she said, 'I can't, because my husband and I are in the ministry.' I questioned her further on this and asked her why she couldn't do both. After all, God had placed those desires in her heart, so maybe he would allow her to be in ministry and fulfil her other aspirations as well.

That lady had a side to her that had been locked up; there was a whole area of gifting inside her life that she had never fully explored and it could have been so fruitful for God if she had expressed it. More than that, it would have moved her further on her identity journey. I think it's time to go back to the drawing board and rethink how we try to define who people are.

Otherwise, we will keep boxing people in, instead of helping them break free from their identity crisis.

Identity theft

Identity theft has become one of the fastest growing crimes around the world. It occurs when the theft of your personal information takes place and someone else uses it to access your finances. A recent TV programme on this subject explained that one in four rubbish bins contains important personal information — things like old bank statements, credit card information and utility bills. People throw this stuff away without even thinking about it. All a criminal needs to do is have a quick rummage through the garbage and they can find the information they need to steal someone else's identity. As I watched this programme, I felt God whisper into my spirit, 'Charlotte this is a widespread problem in my church'; As God spoke that into my heart, I felt the sadness that he must feel to see so many of his awesome, original creations living less than awesome, copycat lifestyles.

It must grieve him that rather than work on our own potential, we would try to take a short cut and steal somebody else's identity. We are personally responsible for what God has put in us, yet I think many of his gifts are being wasted. Many people are ignoring the value of what they already have and are trying to create a counterfeit copy of what others have instead.

Identity Crisis

It's much easier to steal someone else's identity than to spend time trying to find out who you are. Just turn on any Christian TV channel and you will see identity theft in action; people who are preaching stolen messages, using stolen mannerisms and even dressing and speaking like other preachers. It's time we called it what it is. It is identity theft and there is no substitute for you being you! We don't want one flavour of preaching or one flavour of church. We need to stop stealing and start travelling; we need to start moving towards who we are called to be. Jacob stole Esau's identity but it didn't get him where he thought it would get him. There were consequences for this theft and there will be consequences for any identities that we try to steal. Counterfeits may look and sound like the real thing at first, but they lack value, they lack substance, they lack originality and eventually, they will be found out.

Sadly, there is widespread identity theft in the church. It is seen where one church tries to steal the identity of another. Rather than finding out who they are and what their church should look like, they try to copy what other churches have spent years pioneering and working for, in the hope that it will give them a quick-fix remedy for their own growth problems. Although it is right to learn from those who are further along on their journey than we are, it is wrong when we try to make an exact copy. God has an individual identity for every single church, but you have to work to find it. Stealing someone else's identity will never get you the results God intended for your community.

We must all go on our own journey — just like Jacob did — to discover who we are and to embrace the identity that God has created for us. Jacob was someone who tried to get away with identity theft but soon discovered that there was no substitute for the genuine thing.

It always saddens me that people, like Jacob, are not valued for who they are. He was unfairly compared to his brother, even though their looks and personalities were completely different. Indeed, personality is an area that I think has often been neglected and unappreciated in the House of God but it is something we need to cherish about each other. It is part of what makes you 'you', and embracing it will help you paint the world with even more of your unique God-colours. So, let's explore the personality factor a little, as we continue on this identity journey together.

Chapter 3

Breaking the Mould

Your personality is what distinguishes you from everyone else; it makes you stand out from the crowd. It makes you different from your best friend, your work colleague or neighbour. Some people, by personality, are funny; they can make you laugh without even trying, whereas others are more melancholy. Certain people can light up a room with their smile and warmth. Others are quiet and gentle compared to the more extrovert, over the top and excitable types. We often think that having a good education or background can give us an advantage in life over other people but more often it's what you as an individual have to offer that makes the biggest difference. Your personality is what attracts certain people and things into your life over others.

Too often we have made people dilute their personalities in order to be accepted in church. We've all seen it; a person gets saved and within six months they have lost their sense of humour, are far less excitable, have toned down their dress sense to something more sensible and to be honest, they have become really boring compared with who they were! God wired you a certain way for a reason. While we believe that everyone needs to work on their lives, because we are all on a journey, we don't want you to kiss goodbye to what makes you 'you!' If you're creative, more contemplative, loud or quiet, that's fine, we just want to allow you to be yourself. Christ is calling us to centre our lives in him and harness our emotions, not to have a personality bypass. Yet many people seem to have forgotten this. Being a follower of Christ should open you up as a person, not shut you down. His House should liberate the real you, not imprison it and his family should be as diverse as his creation.

Jesus loved different personalities. Just look at the disciples to see this; they were a completely diverse group of guys with different gifts and backgrounds. He didn't expect them to conform to an ideal of what a disciple should be like; he didn't want them all to be the same but worked with their individuality.

For example, look at Peter the passionate, who was hot-headed and over the top and John, who was trusting, loyal, calm with great qualities which made him a close friend and confidant. Jesus even made room for people that many of us would choose to do without, like Thomas who could be negative, questioning and over-analytical and Judas, who stole and betrayed him. All of them had the same training from Jesus and were sent out on the same mission but it was their personalities that made them stand out in varying situations and get different responses. Peter could rally the crowd and John could calm them down. I am sure Jesus could have found people who were a lot easier to mould and shape, but instead he chose contrasting characters. All the disciples were involved in the team in a way that suited their individual gifts and abilities. They were all very different, and Jesus celebrated that in them, he didn't try to change them. He didn't want a grey 'elephant' but a multicoloured one, so he chose a team that would give him that.

When I was at school, we were all expected to have a week of work experience during the year. At the age of sixteen, some of us had a clear idea of what we wanted to be while others were completely clueless. I was somewhere in between. I remember sitting with my career adviser as he asked me where I wanted my week long work placement to be. I was interested in media and was drawn to the whole area of communication, so I suggested that I would like to work for the BBC. I remember telling the career adviser that, because of my interests, this would be a fitting placement for me. He wasted no time in telling me that this would not be possible, because there were no placements available at the BBC. Instead of encouraging me to go after something that suited who I was, he tried to make me tone down the colour of my life to fit with what he thought were more acceptable and realistic suggestions.

'Wouldn't you rather do administration work in a local office or help out in the local hospital for a week instead?' he asked. I went home feeling very disheartened because I was being pushed into doing something that just did not interest me.

When I told my mum and dad that my work placement was going to be in an office, helping with secretarial tasks, the lack of excitement in my voice was a clear indication to them that this was not what I really wanted. So, that afternoon, my dad and I made a few phone calls and arranged my own work placement, which included two days with the BBC and another two with a local radio station. They were the same places my career adviser had told me I would never get a placement! Fortunately I was strong enough to question his advice and hold out for something that was more in keeping with my personality. Many people, however, don't speak up. Rather than looking for an alternative, they allow their real identity to be locked up by conforming to the status quo. This can happen to people at any age, not just at sixteen but up to sixty-six and beyond. If you don't know who you are then other people will try to define you.

I am increasingly aware that, as you read this book, you may feel your emotions rising. You may be getting a little 'hot under the collar' as you start thinking about some of the things you are doing, and roles you have in life, which you have taken on without ever thinking about the process I am describing. That's good! God wants you to rethink some things as part of your identity journey. It's never too late to take control of your life.

I have now had the awesome privilege of being involved in the placement of people in our church team and in the hiring and positioning of our staff. I never want to hinder any of them the way my career adviser hindered me. However, it's a real possibility that can happen if I don't take the time to find out people's personalities and think about where they would be best placed. I am constantly looking at our team and reassessing where each one is placed. Sometimes we change the position of our staff three or four times until we find the place that suits them one hundred percent.

We need to make sure we understand and allow for personality when we put people into roles and positions. In our leadership team we have many gifted people who are very capable and can fulfil many roles and carry out many different tasks. Their personality helps us determine which position suits them best. One of our associate pastors, Stephen Matthew, has the office next door to mine and we are a complete contrast. Personality wise he is strong, quiet and intellectual, whereas I am loud and gregarious; always-in-a-rush and getting involved in everything. We have an intercom system in our offices that I never use, because it's much easier to shout through the wall! I'm sure that sometimes Stephen, being more of a quiet, thoughtful type, must wish I would calm down, yet we have learned to embrace and enjoy the difference between us. When we work together on projects, we get the best of both worlds and our personalities, as well as our gifts, are allowed to bring an extra dimension to the team. We have learned to blend and compliment our very different colours. He gets to be himself and I get to be myself.

Similarly, you don't want everyone on your team to have the same personality as the pastor because this would be overwhelming. Sometimes it can seem easier to have people around you who are just like you, because they will react like you and think in a similar way. At first this may seem like a good way to avoid the stress of sorting out personality clashes but if your entire team is very introverted and has a careful approach to life, or if they are all excitable and run head first into situations, then you are going to have problems. You will have a very one-dimensional approach to everything you do. Different personalities spark off each other but when they are harnessed together in the right way, they bring richness to the team. They bring a wealth of ideas and approaches to different situations that are invaluable. That's why we must commit to letting people be themselves and hire them with that in mind.

Casting directors

If we don't allow for individual personalities, many wrong calls will be made in the workplace, in relationships and in our church environments. A misunderstanding of this journey of identity can make over-zealous people attempt to tidy up where they think others should fit in life. Potentially, they will try to force people to be something they were never intended to be.

In the life of a church there are many different roles to fullfil and leaders can end up feeling like the casting directors of church life because they have to put people into the various roles that need to be filled. But just like in a movie, if the wrong actor gets chosen for a certain role, it can ruin the whole film. Sometimes there are people in churches who are definitely in the wrong role and it becomes obvious that they don't have what it takes to play that particular part. As a result, some Christians spend years of their lives unhappy and unfullfilled because they were wrongly placed. They start to doubt themselves, and when they realise they don't have the ability to fullfil the demands of the role cast for them, their confidence is eroded. However, if they are placed in a position that suits them, they flourish and start having the time of their lives.

In the New Testament, Paul uses the illustration of a body to show how we are all different parts of the same whole. He says, *'If the whole body were an eye, where would the sense of hearing be? If the whole body were an ear, where would the sense of smell be? But in fact God has arranged the parts in the body, every one of them, just as he wanted them to be. If they were all one part, where would the body be? As it is, there are many parts, but one body.'* (1 Corinthians 12:17-20)

It may seem obvious but you are going to struggle if your physical body parts are not in the right place. Yet when churches put people in the wrong roles, it is like trying to make parts of Christ's body function in a way that they were not designed to. We need to think seriously about this, because the consequences of a wrong casting affects far more people than just that individual. Everyone else who works alongside them, including the staff team and wider church family, will also feel the effects and that is why it is important to get it right. Sometimes we need to stop, watch what is going on around us and think about whether some people need repositioning so the real 'them' can come out.

As part of our Leadership Academy course, we spend time helping our students to find out more about their identity and where they fit in life. One of the exercises I do with the class helps them assess their leadership strengths and weaknesses. It was during one of these assessments that a young man on the course, who felt very unfulfilled in his job in the caring profession, had a sudden realisation that he had spent the first ten working years of his life in the wrong field. His real self was not drawn to the caring profession. It was just not what he enjoyed doing and as a result, he felt like a real failure. When he started to really think about who he was and his personality, he discovered that he didn't like working with people and their problems, he actually enjoyed working alone. In fact, the way he was wired meant that he loved working on things that required technical skills and expertise. Today he works in a completely different career and is excelling in a job that is suited to his real self. This shows how much it is possible to achieve when you put your energy in the right place, and refuse to get locked into roles that don't suit you.

Be yourself

My mum, Glenda, is an amazing woman and one of my best friends. I have watched her many times over the years as people have tried to create an identity for her. They have tried to put her in a slot that she just wasn't designed for. Being a pastor's wife meant that many people thought that she should have a public ministry. Says who? I love my mum's confidence in knowing who she is. She used to be intimidated by the pressure put on her to fit a mould called the 'pastors wife', where she would be expected to dress, act and speak in a certain way. Over the years, she has been on a journey and come to the place where her identity is not a crisis point for her. Today, when people question what she does, she responds confidently, because she has learned to be secure in who she is, not in who people think she should be.

Glenda is an extremely talented and gifted lady, involved in many things in our church world. She is faithful and loyal, a great supporter, friend and lover of people but she will not, and does not want to be a public speaker. The invitations still come for her to speak, simply because she is married to a well known preacher but now, when the invitations come for Paul to speak and they ask, 'Could your wife speak too?' she simply replies, 'No, that's not me!' She once explained it like this. If you had a leak and called out a plumber, and his wife answered the phone and said, 'I am sorry, but my husband is out,' would you ask, 'Can you come instead?' It would be ridiculous to assume that the wife is a plumber just because she is married to one! But we put these expectations on each other in church all the time. If you aren't confident in who you are, then you can end up being called out to fix leaks, without the ability to do the job and end up making matters much worse!

My mum's journey has been a great inspiration to me, She gave me an alternative model to follow, which I drew upon in my first few years of marriage to Steve when I faced a similar dilemma of living up to other people's expectations. At the time, we were in a network of churches where ministry was pretty much synonymous with being a man and we ladies were the support act. When we first started to date, Steve was a youth pastor in the local church, and the understanding was that if *he* loved youth ministry, then so must *I*. The problem was, I didn't. After getting married we fell into a routine where every Friday night, I would attend the youth meeting to support Steve. I have to say, I went along with this for a while but eventually the real me started to speak up. The truth was I really didn't enjoy youth ministry. I thought it was too loud, I didn't want to spend my time picking up rubbish after a bunch of teenagers and I just didn't enjoy all the crazy stuff they all seemed to thrive on. Eventually, this started to cause friction in our marriage. Every Friday night our house was full of stress. I'd get home from work and be told to hurry up so we could leave for the youth meeting. I would protest, saying I didn't want to go. Steve would talk me into it and then, for the entire ride in the car, I would nag about how I didn't want to be out late, how I was tired and I certainly wasn't going to be picking up empty coke cans again! Poor Steve then had to get out of the car and find the energy to overcome his wife's bad attitude and inspire the young people. It was certainly a bumpy ride for a while, until one day the real me spoke up and said, 'I'm not coming to youth anymore. I don't like it and I don't want to go!' Steve knew that other people would think something was wrong if I didn't go, they would think I was an unsupportive wife, but inside his heart he knew he needed to release me. I think he also realised how stress-free his Fridays would be if he left me at home!

Instead of being the 'youth pastor's wife', I started to concentrate on getting out what was inside of me. I went on my own journey to find out what I was built to do. Before long, I was involved in a variety of different areas in the church that were more in keeping with who I was. As I got involved in things I was good at, my confidence grew and I began to achieve more. Where I had been reluctant to be involved in the young peoples' ministry, I found I had a passion for other areas. A passion I probably would never have discovered, if I had not set off on this journey. I would have remained stuck under the confines of a label that didn't even fit me, feeling I had failed, rather than moving forward into areas where I could excel.

Some people said I should have stuck with my husband and shown my support but we have been able to reach more people between us, as a couple, by releasing each other to soar with our strengths and callings. The friction disappeared from our marriage as we both started to enjoy what we were doing. It implies in Deuteronomy 32:30 that one man can put a thousand to flight but two put ten thousand to flight and this is what we have seen happen through our lives. We have a greater combined impact as a couple, now that we are both doing what God has called us to. I have told this story in several different settings around the world and every time I have had people come afterwards and say, 'That's me; I am trapped in this role and don't know what to do!'

If you want a happy marriage, if you want great friendships, if you want a great life and if you want to grow your church, then release each other to be who you really are. The only thing you will lose is the stress and with it you will find a new level of fulfilment in watching each other grow and flourish. Sometimes I wonder what we are keeping locked up. What are we keeping trapped under titles, roles and descriptions that could be changing our world if we let it loose?

Submission

I feel at this point that I need to clarify one thing. I don't want you to be reading this book and thinking I am advocating anarchy in your church, marriage or workplace. This journey is not one of rebellion; it is one of submission. I am not encouraging you to suddenly throw your hands in the air and resign from your job saying, 'this isn't me. I was not created to be a shop assistant or a bank manager.' I'm not, for a moment, suggesting that you stop helping at church, saying, 'God simply didn't create me to put the chairs out, or be on the welcome team, or serve in Kid's church. I'm out of here!'

What I am saying is, don't let yourself be locked into something you are doing today, because your future may look different. However, we all need guidance and wisdom on our journey and that comes from staying planted in God's House. We have to be in a place of submission. We need to have our hearts and lives submitted to God and to his word. I didn't rebel and leave youth ministry. I didn't give my husband an ultimatum, because my heart was in complete submission to him. As a couple we have discovered that submission is a two-way partnership. Although God requires the woman, in a marriage, to submit to her husband, he also requires the husband to love her, as Christ loves the church (Eph 5:22-33). This picture of submission shows a two-way relationship, where one person lays down their life and the other handles it carefully — as if it were a precious jewel. This is the way that submission should work in the church, marriage, friendships and in every other scenario. When we love people in this way, they will have no problem submitting to the wisdom and guidance of those who lead them. When someone loves you like Christ, submission is easy, because you are safe in their counsel. They are not your jailers. They are your freedom fighters and they want you to be 'you', because that's what Christ wants for you.

Submission only becomes difficult when one part of the deal is broken. Too many people are staying trapped, doing something that does not suit who they really are, because they think it would be wrong or rebellious to move away from the confinement of that role. Yet, if the person who is keeping you in that role is not loving and nurturing your life, it is not a fair exchange. We must be very careful that we don't ask people to submit to things that God wouldn't ask them to submit to and that we always act out of a genuine love and concern for them. If we don't, people will sometimes be faced with the difficult situation of feeling they must 'move on', because they simply can't be 'themselves' with all the constraints that have been placed on their lives. We only have one life to live and we cannot afford to spend our time living beneath our full potential because of false loyalties. We have to 'break the mould' and keep moving.

God understands that the journey to finding your identity is not always easy but you are not alone. He has given you the Holy Spirit as your travelling companion, to help you determine where you are going. We need to have lives that are tuned into his frequency, so that his guidance acts as our inner compass and leads us in the right direction on our identity journey.

Chapter 4

Instinct

As you travel on your identity journey, you need to be tuned in to the God-given help of the Holy Spirit; he is there to help you. This was something Jesus made sure his disciples understood before he left them. Jesus told them that, *'the Counsellor, the Holy Spirit, whom the Father will send in my name, will teach you all things and will remind you of everything I have said to you' (John 14:26)*. The Holy Spirit was not an afterthought, he was part of God's purpose and plan for helping every child of God get through their journey in life. It is like God has given you an onboard satellite navigation system. As you continue on your journey, this God-given help needs to be engaged and must be fully operational in your life if you are to maximise the purpose for which it was given to you.

Although you have it onboard, you may never have taken the time to learn how to use it. The Holy Spirit plays a vital role in helping you take the right route. It will get you through periods when all the clear road signs have been removed and the road markings are not even visible. The internal promptings of the Holy Spirit are fully accessible and able to guide you, even when you are feeling lost and disorientated, because he knows every bump on the road and every unexpected twist and turn that you will face. Once you realise this and learn to journey with him, you will become less dependent on external signposts to tell you where to go next.

The Holy Spirit operates in many ways — one of which is through your instinct. Your instinct is your inner God-prompting; it is the whispering and nudging of the Holy Spirit to your heart. Your instinct is that gut feeling you get about a situation or a person; it's that 'knowing' you have on the inside that comes from God leading you. However, too often we refer to everywhere and everyone else before we engage the help we really need.

On my journey, I have had to learn to trust my God-given instinct. When I follow it, I gain confidence and step closer to being the person God wants me to be. It has guided me through many situations It has helped me say no to 'Rebekah' when she has entered my world, and it has made me speak up or shut up at the right moments. Following my instinct has freed me from trying to second guess God or seek the approval and permission of other people before I step out. It's unique to my journey; it's tailor made to my circumstances and leads me towards the person God wants me to be.

Staying in step

Learning to follow your God-given instinct will help you build a life that keeps in step with God. It says in Galatians, *'Since we live by the Spirit, let us keep in step with the Spirit.' (5:25)* Keeping in step with the spirit is only possible when we remain tuned in, with the volume fully turned up, on our internal 'satellite navigation system'. Just stepping out in the Spirit is not enough. Often we can find the courage to step out and start moving on this journey but then we gradually drift out of step. We get distracted; we are no longer listening with the same intensity that was required to get us moving in the first place. It's not enough to know the first few steps needed. Galatians tells us we have to live our whole life in step. If you want to be in step with God, then you have to walk closely with him and you need to follow his every move. When our lives are out of step with the Holy Spirit, it is like doing the tango while he is trying to lead us in a waltz! Somehow we need to align our life with his and remove any hindrances that are stopping us from following his steps.

Living your life out of step will not make you a bad person. It will not prevent you from having eternal life but it will slow you down on the journey to becoming one hundred percent 'you'. You need to get to a place where you completely trust and listen to his voice and where you are tuned into God's whisper. When this happens, the Holy Spirit becomes your dancing partner. If you dance with someone who has 'two left feet', they become like a lead weight and instead of leading you around the dance floor, you have to drag them around with you; and the whole experience can be quite painful and embarrassing. However, when you watch a couple who are perfectly in step with one another, it looks so graceful. They glide, it's beautiful and no-one is screaming 'ouch' as their partner lands on their foot for the third time!

What does your journey with God look like? Is he dragging you to discover more of what is in you, or do you keep standing on his toes, because you won't let him lead? Or are you gliding gracefully and keeping up? Are you allowing him to teach you and guide you, or are you doing your own thing? The Holy Spirit wants to lead you, but he won't force you. He will simply prompt you and start the dance. It's then your job to follow and keep up.

We need to make our lives easy to manoeuvre on this journey. We need to allow the power of the Holy Spirit's instinct inside us to have a voice. Can you trust this instinct for direction, or do you need seven signs and wonders before you will consider changing step? The problem for many is that they have become too enamoured with a certain style of steps. If you love the waltz and the Holy Sprit is instinctively telling you it is time to tango, I have news for you today. It's not his job to compromise and slow down, it's your job to quickly learn to love the tango! Speed up your journey; take quicker and bigger steps. The Holy Spirit is your personal choreographer; he knows the right steps and the right tempo for your unique journey. He knows what dance you were created to do. That's why wasting time, going round in circles, listening to and following everyone else's lead, will only wear you out without taking you any further forward.

Before I go on, I just want to say that following your instinct doesn't mean kissing your brains goodbye, throwing your diary out of the window and living by your feelings! I am a very organised person and my friends even laugh at me because of it. If I am speaking at a conference, I plan all my outfits before I set off. I know what I am wearing each day before I arrive. I just haven't got time to worry about it later. I want to know that everything is dry cleaned, in my suitcase and ready to go. I appreciate and find it necessary to have an organised life in order to do all I feel God has called me to do. I have to constantly be careful though, that I don't organise myself out of step with God. I've had to learn how to tune into those God promptings and every time, it has taken me on an unexpected twist on the journey of discovering who I am. I could list many incidents where God has whispered things into my heart and they have become a catalyst for a complete re-routing of where I thought I was heading. Where I had planned to go was okay but where God had planned for me to go was far better. The destination I had set out for was linked to who I thought I should be but his destination for my life was about who he knew I was created to be.

God's master production

There are different people God wants to connect your life to at particular points on your journey, instead of just sticking with the people you have around you.

You are not called to dance solo; your life is not a one-man show. You are actually part of a master production and God is the author and director of everything that is happening. Right now you can only see your lines, but God has the full script in front of him. There are other people who he will bring across your path who you need to interact with. He sees all the people you are supposed to have a dialogue with and everyone you are going to be in a scene with. He knows who will play a long-term role in your life and those who will make a cameo appearance. He has planned the scenery, lighting and costume changes and knows the plot from beginning to end.

The Holy Spirit is like a prompt at the side of your life who is trying to get your attention for your next cue. He knows that when you walk across the stage, the person heading towards you is someone you need to have a conversation with and they are there by design not coincidence. We need to learn to follow his prompting so that what needs to be said is said and what he wants done is done.

I saw this unfold before my eyes recently for a young man named Jason. The beginning of his journey came from an 'instinct' moment along my path. One Christmas time, I felt that our women's ministry, Flourish, should bless young teenagers who were leaving local authority care to live independently. So we put together luxury gift hampers and invited some of the youngsters to come and pick them up from the church campus. This was a God prompting but I had no idea it was going to be all about this one guy. His identity had been shaped over the years by many difficult circumstances. He had been moved from foster home to foster home, suffered abuse and lived a life of adversity and hardship. In his own eyes he was worthless. He had turned to crime and carried out a number of serious offences. Most people would describe him as one of life's losers. Jason was soon to face a court hearing to find out how long his prison sentence would be.

I met Jason when he came to pick up his hamper and felt drawn to speak to him. I was drawn past his hard exterior and let God lead me beyond my own pre-conceptions and apprehensions in speaking to him. Jason came back to a church service later that week and got saved. A few weeks later we baptised him just before he was due to go for sentencing.

Within a short space of time Jasons' perception of who he was totally transformed. He even went to the police to confess over forty additional crimes he had committed, because he felt God had challenged him about becoming a new creation. People that were assigned to watch over Jason, from police officers to social workers, were all astounded as this other person, this new identity evolved and was expressed. On the day Jason was to be sentenced, his barrister explained to the judge how there had been a dramatic change in his client and how attending church had given him a completely different outlook on life. What happened next for Jason was a complete intervention by God.

Amazingly, the judge let him go free because he could not reconcile the offences with the new person Jason had become. He could see that being in a different environment and having people around him to support and encourage him had helped him become a different person. The case made the local news and we were contacted for an explanation of how a person could change so drastically and suddenly have a different identity.

Jason has taken the first few steps on his identity journey; already he has started to understand more about who he is in Christ, he is changing his relationships and altering his values. He now has a new destination in life. Jason has started to understand that his identity was not in any of the labels life had handed him. He didn't have to be a victim, a criminal or a tear-away. He could be whatever he dreamed of being and in finding Christ he found a place to bring those dreams alive. Jason now wants to learn, see and do new things, all in keeping with who he always really was.

Jason was a brief encounter on my own journey. His journey was always destined to cross with mine but we both had to be obedient to our God given instinct and follow those promptings in order to connect. He had to respond to the invitation and I had to be obedient to extend that invitation. Now our paths have moved on again and Jason has connected his life with other people who are helping him on the next phase of his journey. We have to learn to respond, to engage and when the time comes, to move on whenever God prompts us. It's called 'staying in step' and by doing so, many people find out who they truly are.

We see a similar pattern in the lives of Christ's disciples when they were suddenly faced with an enormous challenge — feeding five thousand people! This incident served to help their identity journeys unfold a little more. Some were immediately obedient to following their instinct, while others were more reluctant. We read that: *'When Jesus looked up and saw a great crowd coming toward him, he said to Philip, "Where shall we buy bread for these people to eat?" He asked this only to test him, for he already had in mind what he was going to do. Philip answered him, "Eight months' wages would not buy enough bread for each one to have a bite!" Another of his disciples, Andrew, Simon Peter's brother spoke up, "Here is a boy with five small barley loaves and two small fish, but how far will they go among so many?"'(John 6:5-9)*

Challenging situations like this often uncover who we really are. Sometimes we can try to cover up where we are at but as soon as we are put under pressure it will come out.

That day Philip had doubts and the real 'him' was exposed when he spoke from his insecurity and negativity. Andrew was a different character. He had enough confidence to make a suggestion and went with the prompting he felt. Yet God didn't write Philip off, as he knew he was on a journey and this negativity would not be the thing that defined him forever. As he continued on his journey, a different Philip began to emerge. In Acts 8, after Jesus had left and the Holy

Spirit was prompting Philip, we see him have the courage and the trust to not doubt but to move out:

'Now an angel of the Lord said to Philip, "Go south to the road — the desert road — that goes down from Jerusalem to Gaza." So he started out, and on his way he met an Ethiopian eunuch, an important official in charge of all the treasury of Candace, queen of the Ethiopians. This man had gone to Jerusalem to worship, and on his way home was sitting in his chariot reading the book of Isaiah the prophet. The Spirit told Philip, "Go to that chariot and stay near it." Then Philip ran up to the chariot and heard the man reading the book of Isaiah the prophet. "Do you understand what you are reading?" Philip asked. "How can I" he said, "unless someone explains it to me?" So he invited Philip to come up and sit with him.' (Acts 8:26-31)

Not only had Philip discovered how to keep in step with the Spirit and follow his instincts, he dramatically affected the identity journey of the Ethiopian. He was an influential government official, released to discover more of his true identity in Christ. I sometimes wonder just what happened next for him and who he went on to help.

You may think you are a negative person — but maybe that isn't the real 'you' and Christ in you can change you. Don't ever write yourself off and make excuses for your behaviour by saying it's because of your family background or it's just the way you are. Your journey isn't over yet — or maybe yours hasn't even started! When you begin to find your identity, like Andrew and Philip you will find yourself stepping out with confidence from the label you once wore. You will realise that things you thought were impossible for someone like you are now entirely possible.

There are many things I have had to remove or silence in my world and uncouple myself from, to enable me to go on my journey and empower the voice of my instinct. These are things we must all deal with and some people are only 'one step' away from discovering more about their true selves.

Only an excuse away

How many times has an excuse stopped you from following your instinct? Are you someone who has a tendency to say, 'I can't do that because . . .!' 'I can't' is the language of excuses, and you will always be able to find plenty of reasons to stop you from following what is in your heart. Have you ever been just about to say something but stopped yourself because you didn't want to upset anyone? Inside, you were really annoyed about something, but decided to just smile rather than cause a fuss by letting that person know what you really thought. By not expressing the real 'you', you are keeping your life on pause. Many people are locked up emotionally and mentally, because for years they have not had the courage to express who they are. They never stood up to the bully; they never spoke out at the injustice. We don't need any more Christians to live this double life. We need them to start listening to their instinct and learning how to be who they are in grace, stature and wisdom. If you are constantly giving what you think are valid reasons for your lack of progress on your journey, then be careful, because eventually your life will grind to a halt. You will end up spending years of your life in a dead end called 'excuses', and the only person responsible for putting you there, is you!

Many people have tried to excuse themselves out of their God-given destiny. There was Moses, whose image of himself was as a poor communicator and Gideon, who saw himself as a weakling, when his true self was a mighty warrior. Then there was Elijah, who hid in the desert — a place that was not on the route God had given him. He reeled off a long list of excuses to God about why he was there. After all, the rest of the Israelites had rejected God and if that wasn't enough, Queen Jezebel was trying to kill him! God wasn't impressed by his excuses and simply said, 'What are you doing here Elijah?' Then God told him to go back the way he came!

Your excuses will never change God's mind about who you are. He sees past your excuses to the real you. All they will do is make your journey far longer than necessary and you will waste time taking pointless detours and delay finding out what God has for your life. So whatever your favourite excuse is, you need to push past it and step out, because your excuses are hiding the real you!

Too busy to fit you in

Or is it busyness? Sometimes life can get so busy that

we are rushing through days and weeks trying to get through a list of tasks without stopping to re-evaluate our lives. It's important to stop sometimes and think about why you are doing what you do. Why are you involved in that particular ministry? Why are you still in the job you dislike so much? Why haven't you gone back to college to study that subject you are interested in? Are you busy with the priorities God has for your life, or are you just cramming your life full of activity? You may be doing some great things with your time but are they stretching you, growing your life and taking you closer to being one hundred percent you and accomplishing what you were put on this planet to do?

Once I was teaching some of the women in the church. I asked them to draw a ladder and place at the top the things they value and spend time on and at the bottom what they spent the least time on. I then gave them words like home, husband, church, friends and children and asked them to place them on the ladder in order of importance. Finally, I told them to place themselves on that priority list. Many of them put themselves either at the bottom of the ladder, or there was no space left to fit themselves in! This told me their own lives were not a high priority to them and it is a common problem. We can be so busy valuing everyone else that our own journey gets put on hold. Yet all our busyness can never ultimately replace the progress we would have made, if we just took the time to work on ourselves and our own journeys.

I have had to learn, as I embrace more responsibility, that I need to keep redefining my priorities. I may have a list of seven tasks to get through but God is looking at number five and is digging me in the ribs saying, 'You need to do that one first. I know it doesn't look important, but you can't see what I see right now!' I have had to learn to respond whenever that happens.

Many of us need to learn to streamline our time and start saying 'no' to tasks that are not a God priority for our lives. It is too easy to live life at breakneck speed being very busy without being productive. Everything we do should be leading us closer to who we are and if it doesn't, then we need to re-evaluate our lives. Don't let yourself get so stuck in the routine of life that you don't hear God whispering to your heart and nudging you in a particular direction in life. There are many things you can be too busy for but the Holy Spirit should never be one of them.

Can't get up

One of the devil's greatest tools for hijacking your journey is comfort. He wants you to be so comfortable that you curl up in the armchair of your life and refuse to move. An armchair is one of the hardest places to move from, especially if it's raining and miserable outside. Staying put, with a cup of coffee and watching your favourite TV show, is always a more attractive option. We can be like this in our spiritual life, but being in a comfortable place is not good for us. It can lead to spiritual laziness and if this takes a hold of your life, you will lose interest in going any further on your journey. Many Christians have done this and have put their journey 'on hold' while they cocoon themselves in the comfortable surroundings of church life, their family or friendships.

An armchair lifestyle will prevent you from discovering anything more about yourself; it is the equivalent of taking spiritual retirement. I have been amazed at how many middle-aged people think their identity journey has finished, they have stopped travelling and are now lounging around in comfort with their feet up. When I talk to them, I sense how much more there is for them to discover, do and see. Often, they are so comfortable in their role of leader, mother, employer, employee, or in the level they find themselves at in life, that they have no desire to go any further. There is no such thing as 'retirement mode' with God and if you think he has finished with you, then it must be time for you to go home! Or maybe, it's actually time for you to climb back out of that armchair. It's time to lose your 'laid back' attitude, to stir up his passion in your heart, to get moving again, to leave your comfort zone behind and get back on the road.

Moses had retired at the age of eighty. His retirement plan was a nice place on the hill, away from people, looking after a far less demanding flock of sheep. Delivering a nation from slavery and leading millions of people was nowhere to be found in his retirement plan. Looking after sheep was his plan, taking life easy was his plan and slowing down was his plan. He soon discovered that God's plan was the complete opposite. Moses was going from a 'slow waltz' to 'break dancing' at the grand old age of eighty! So I say to any eighty plus year olds reading this book, be careful what you plan, because maybe your journey is only just beginning! To all those under eighty, if you have already climbed into your armchair, then I must warn you that God won't let you rest. If Moses couldn't do that at eighty years old, you have no excuse to start getting comfortable. The real Moses had not even started to come out until this late stage in his life. The real Moses wasn't a follower, but a leader; the real Moses wasn't scared but strong; the real Moses wasn't inarticulate but eloquent; the real Moses was not designed to shepherd sheep but to lead three million people. All of this only emerged as he embarked on his journey. These awesome leadership qualities, the strength and the courage to take on Pharaoh, lay undiscovered until he got in step with God once more.

If you are currently living a cosy existence in your comfort zone, then it is time to get some momentum back in your life and in order to do this, you are going to have to remove some 'stabilisers'. Leaving your comfort zone will grow you and stretch you as you trust your inner instinct and step out into the unknown. It will help you discover so much more about what God has put in your life.

I experienced this when I first went on a ministry trip and had to leave behind the familiarity and comfort zone of being at my home church. When I was speaking at home it was much easier. Everyone I loved was there and I could predict how the church would respond to me. This time I was alone and I had to leave everything that was familiar behind. It was an unsettling experience but God needed to get me on my own to show me what was in my life and to affirm in me that my identity journey was not finished yet. That was what Jacob's journey was about — he had to leave the comfort zone of his mother to discover how much more there was out there for him. Without the 'stabiliser' of his mother's voice and direction, he could still make it; and, in fact, he would be a lot better off.

So today, as you read this, are you sitting in your armchair or in the safety of your comfort zone? If so, please don't just gloss over these words. Let them penetrate your heart and let this challenge cause you to get moving and continue with your journey. Maybe you were once on this journey but with it came pain and confrontation and you grazed your knee as the 'stabilisers' came off! As a result, you retreated back into the comfort of your 'armchair', just as Moses did after the incident when he killed an Egyptian feeling disorientated, confused and having let God down. He went back to an 'armchair' style life. Don't do the same, or your armchair will become your prison.

It says in 2 Timothy, *'For this reason I remind you to fan into flame the gift of God, which is in you.'* (1:6) The responsibility for kick-starting and maintaining your spiritual momentum lies with you. You need to choose to live differently, to start listening to your instinct and tune back in to the 'nudgings' of the Holy Spirit in your life.

Instinct

You may feel like you have two left feet you may think that you are so 'out of practice' that you will never be able to keep in step with him again but be encouraged. Remove the excuses, get up and live your life — not someone else's. What's stopping you? Identify it, address it and if necessary separate from it. Do whatever it takes to become the real you. Have the guts to get up and journey on.

Chapter 5

Separation

Your identity journey is one of both connection and separation. As you walk in step with God, there will be times when he will ask you to separate from anything that is holding you back. Separation is actually a vital stage on your journey. For some it is geographical or relational but for others it means leaving behind certain behaviours, mind sets or comfort zones that stop them moving forward. For Jacob it meant leaving behind the security of his family and setting off into the unknown but this brought him to a place where God could start to reshape his ideas about who he was. In the same way, separation will bring you to a place where God can break into your world and talk to you about the real 'you'.

One of the most significant turning points in Jacob's journey took place as soon as he separated from his mother Rebekah. As he was thrust out on his own he had to separate, not only relationally from his family but also emotionally and geographically. All his reference points were removed and his comfort zone was left far behind. In the dark of the night he lay his head down to sleep, probably feeling very alone, confused and unsettled. It was in this moment that God showed up.

I have discovered that often God doesn't show up when we think he should. For much of the journey he doesn't need to redirect or re-route our lives. The Holy Spirit is not erratic; he doesn't change his mind all the time. He simply wants you to find your step and get into your flow. In order to do that, there will be some key points of separation.

On the very first night of separation, God revealed himself to Jacob in a dream. Jacob woke up saying, *'Surely the Lord is in this place, and I was not aware of it,' (Genesis 28:16)* What seems shocking is that Jacob could be so oblivious to the presence of God Almighty. God had always been there for Jacob but he had failed to recognise his presence for himself because Rebekah had become the dominating frequency he was tuned into. She had become like the voice of God to his life and had become the dictator of his identity; he simply responded to her wishes and nothing of the real Jacob came to the surface. She told him what to do and where to go, and even her parting words to him were about whom he should marry and where he should live. The only way forward for Jacob was separation from her controlling influence; removing this 'stabiliser' brought a new freedom and signalled the start of a new chapter of his life.

Embracing change

Separation and change always go hand in hand. Therefore we must learn not to resist change but embrace it in our world. God will use situations, circumstances and people to get you moving in the right direction again. This is what happened to Jacob: once he left Rebekah behind, his life changed dramatically.

The true identity of this young man, who up until that point had been kept firmly tied to his mother's apron strings, started to emerge. The scriptures describe him as a quiet man (Gen 25:27) but once he separated from his mother, other aspects of his character started to emerge. He was diligent and a hard worker not a shirker or cheat, which soon became evident as he worked long hours minding sheep in the fields. The real Jacob was only let loose once he stopped trying to live the life of his brother and started to be himself.

This time of separation forced him to re-evaluate his life. He had to face up to his past mistakes and choose for himself how he wanted to live. He had every opportunity to carry on the way he had before, because he found himself working for his Uncle Laban who deceived and cheated him on many occasions. He tricked Jacob into marrying Leah instead of Rachel, he kept changing Jacob's wages and was a dishonest man. This was the ultimate test for Jacob because he was faced with the very thing that he himself had battled with. He had been forced to deceive his father and his brother before and now he had to question whether it was a characteristic that he wanted in his life. Jacob discovered he didn't identify with Laban and the way he did life. He was repelled by his uncle's underhanded behaviour and instead, started building a life that was honest and hardworking. He began to work out who he really was and every decision he made not to be like Laban affirmed that in him.

Separation leads to connection

Many people, when they hear the word separation, immediately have thoughts of a negative nature. They think of tension, conflict, loss and hurt, as in their mind, they recall bad experiences where friends or family have separated and the fall-out has been damaging. I want us to consider the possibility that separation can not only be positive but a complete necessity. Whether separation hurts or heals has to do with the way you handle it. I have separated badly from people and situations and I have done it in a way that has brought joy to my life. The difference was not that one separation was easier than another; the difference was that I learned to look at things the way God does.

Separation is a natural process of life. People separate from their parents when they leave to study and a separation of a more permanent nature happens when they get married. Separation can happen when you move jobs or relocate to another part of the country. It's part of everyday life and we need an equivalent understanding in the spiritual realm that separation is a normal part of our journey. If you want to keep discovering what is in you, then you have to learn to separate from anything that no longer fits your identity.

When my husband was growing up in Washington State, America, his parents owned a large restaurant and hotel business. After Steve left high school he had a big decision to make. He could stay and be part of the family business, which would guarantee him a wage and job as soon as school was finished, or he could separate himself from the comforts of his family to pursue other dreams. Steve's home town of Wenatchee is a very beautiful place, but as far as career choices go, it was severely limited. Therefore, if he were to pursue a different career, it would not just mean separation physically, but also geographically. Steve had a dream to pursue music; it was his passion and so, in order to keep getting out what was in his heart, he left the 'stabilisers' of a promised wage and familiar faces to pursue his own unique journey. He left home and went to study at a prestigious Music Academy. Eventually he played with the New York Philharmonic at the Waterloo Festival and the St. Louis Symphony Orchestra as a percussionist.

While he was on that journey, he met Christ and after all the hard work he had put in over the years to get to the very top of his chosen field, he faced another challenge of separation. All that he had worked for no longer satisfied the real Steve and his journey was about to take a new direction as he began to pursue more of God; he had to go through another separation.

This step took him to the other side of the world to Bible College in the UK, which brought him into my world. The momentum in his world, caused by separation, connected him to new relationships that were part of God's plan for his life. I for one, am extremely grateful that he had the guts to separate again, from all he knew and had built up over the years, because through his diligence of separation our future together became a possibility. It makes me wonder how many others God has tried to move along. He knows what they need and desire is further down the road but their reluctance to separate means they never get what they are sitting at home praying for.

So, instead of thinking separation is something to fear, we should realise that separation is something to embrace. For Jacob, the separation from his mother eventually led him to meet Rachel, the love of his life but along the way he had to watch out for Leah. She was his opportunity to once again go 'out of step'. He could have said at this point, 'I have journeyed far enough so I'm going to settle for second best'. He refused to do that and instead handled the confrontation with Laban and the upheaval of leaving Rebekah in order to stay true to his heart's desire. He kept going instead of settling. What about you?

We have had people join our church from all over the world who have had to leave family and friends behind. They have sold their homes and possessions to come to Bradford, which is not exactly in the top ten of the most glamorous places to relocate to. Yet when I have talked to some of these families, their explanation is simply that they felt God say that this separation needed to happen for the next piece of the jigsaw of their lives to fall into place. Since they arrived, they have walked into many God-given connections, unique to their journey, which have helped them discover more about themselves; discoveries that they could have spent ten years praying for.

Sometimes separation can be difficult because it means leaving behind things that we have become very attached to in life. I have a pair of size eight jeans that I enjoy wearing. It took me a lot of hard work and effort on my treadmill to make them fit and I am so pleased that I can fit into them and am still able to breathe! But when I was pregnant I had to separate from my jeans and embrace the new shaped me. Spiritually, this picture is also true-we might like what we have always known, we may want to hold on to what we worked hard to get and what we think looks good on us. However if God has a new thing to birth through our lives, then we are going to have to learn to embrace our new shape and accept the fact that we may never be able to go back to the size we were. The great news is that the benefit of going through the separation will always outweigh the cost, something to which my two beautiful children are a testimony.

So, what do you need to separate from in your life? For some the answer is drastic but for many others the answer is much simpler; it's a separation from wrong thinking about ourselves, a separation from relationships that need to change or a separation from how we perceive certain things.

Tears and tantrums

I have been through some challenging times of separation on my journey. Although I have never separated from my family or locality for any length of time, on many occasions I have had to separate myself internally, mentally and relationally in order to keep growing.

One of these times came when I was faced with separation from a role. When I first went on staff at the church I was personal assistant to my dad, the Senior Pastor, Paul Scanlon. But there came a time when the leadership team felt I had outgrown the role and wanted me to transition onto the next level. There were some massive changes taking place in my world at that time. I was pregnant with my first child, Hope Cherish, and when she was born it meant I had a natural break from the office for several weeks. I came back to work to discover that while I was away even more changes had taken place and that my work world now looked very different. While I was away, they had promoted one of the assistants, Emma, to take over my desk.

To say I didn't take it very well is an understatement. I certainly didn't embrace the change and the separation that came my way willingly. In fact, I caused a complete uproar with my bad attitude and by the way I handled it. I felt so hurt and wondered, How they could replace me so easily? One day I remember marching into Paul's office and saying in a highly dramatic and emotional fashion, 'I can't believe you'd do this to me, I just don't deserve it. I think I'm going to leave because I'm not needed anymore!' I remember to this day, Paul didn't flinch; he didn't even look up from his notes for a second but just said, 'Ok, if that's what you want!' You see the real issue was- what did the real Charlotte really want next?

Despite the tears and tantrums, Paul would not help me answer that question; he simply refused to be like Rebekah to me. No matter how much I pleaded for it, he would not tell me who I should be, where I should go or what I should do. He had removed a 'stabiliser' I hadn't even realised I was so dependent on – the 'stabiliser' of my role. It was what was giving me my identity and security; it made me feel necessary and needed. Now that it had been removed, I was on my own and wobbling badly but he refused to grab the handle bars and steady my ride; he wanted me to learn to ride without assistance He would not give me another role for me to find my identity in. It was something I was going to have to work out for myself. He saw that there was much in my life that I needed to get out and it wasn't going to happen while I was busy working as his PA. He wanted to create space for the real 'me' to be let loose and it took weeks of discussions for me to explore where my natural fit would be as part of the team.

If I'm honest, there came a point in my transition when I knew that, like Jacob, I was taking something that belonged to someone else. The time had come for me to stand aside because I was stopping someone else coming through into that role. I didn't realise that at the time, and responded badly by centering the way I felt on the girl who had replaced me. For a while I saw Emma as the enemy; I thought that it was her fault. I felt this way because she had taken my job! She had taken the thing that defined me and my purpose. Often, when we are struggling to separate from something, it can be easy to blame other people for what is happening. We think that they have caused the problem when actually God is using that person and the circumstance to make you move further on in the journey. This was a time when Emma also got to go further on her journey she gained a new liberty from me moving on.

Too often, in churches, these natural transitions don't happen and you end up with a bottleneck in church life. If someone stays in a role longer than they should for the wrong reasons – for the sake of their security or familiarity – then they hold up the next generation of leaders who should be coming through. Everyone should be on the move. So what about you? Is there movement in your life, or are you stuck? If you are stuck, then realise the change you are dreading is probably the change you need.

During this season, as I struggled with my identity, God said, 'Charlotte, they are not going to give you another role or a job title. This is about you and me and you have to recognise me and what I am doing in you.' As I began to adjust to the changes, new fruit started to come from my life as I started examining what was in my heart and asking myself questions about who I was. I started a women's conference and an event for leaders in our House, I had more time to spend studying God's Word and developing my ability as a speaker. I wrote my first book and had a fresh flow of creativity and new ideas that have blessed our House. The point is, those things were always in me but they were never going to be released until a demand was placed on me to open up and become one hundred percent myself.

If I had understood this at the time, I could have handled it better and not been such an ogre. Maybe you can learn from my mistakes and deliver yourself from the nightmare I gave myself and those around me.

Separation is a season that you will experience at different times during your journey. For Jacob it lasted for twenty years and during this time he made great discoveries about who he was. He left his old identity far behind and connected with his real self and he left old relationships behind and found new ones. It was the start of a long journey dealing with issues in his life that God wanted to talk to him about. His time of separation, the struggle he had working for Laban and the personal challenges he faced as he redefined who he was, were all leading him towards another encounter, where God would ask him a question; a question that was all about his identity.

Chapter 6

What is Your Name?

Jacob became more and more unsettled after many years working for Laban. His circumstances were now very different to when he had first arrived. He had finally married the love of his life, Rachel and they had a family together. He had grown up from being a boy into a man and it was time to separate once more. This time he was to leave behind the uncle that God had used to show him so many things about who he was as a person. One night, God prompted Jacob to change step once again and move on.

This time, Jacob was heading towards a meeting with his brother; he was about to come face to face with Esau. The last time they had spoken, Esau had threatened to take Jacob's life. The thought of their meeting filled Jacob with apprehension, so in order to pacify his brother, he sent herds of animals ahead as gifts. I'm sure, at this point of reconnection, Jacob began to struggle with some of his past mistakes. His brother only knew him as a traitor, a deceiver and a thief and the closer he got to the confrontation with

Esau, the more he was reminded of this old identity. Jacob sent his family and all his possessions across the river ahead of him and God created another identity defining moment. We read, 'So *Jacob was left alone, and a man wrestled with him till daybreak. When the man saw that he could not overpower him, he touched the socket of Jacob's hip so that his hip was wrenched as he wrestled with the man. Then the man said, "'Let me go, for it is daybreak.'" But Jacob replied, "'I will not let you go unless you bless me.'"* (Genesis 32:24-26)

Imagine the scene. Jacob was wrestling throughout the night, wrestling for a blessing which he previously would have stolen. This time it was different, Jacob was determined to be blessed in his own right, for who he was. The most significant part of this wrestle was the question that God asked him; this question was what his entire journey up to that point had been about: '*The man asked him, "What is your name?" "Jacob," he answered. Then the man said, "Your name will no longer be Jacob, but Israel, because you have struggled with God and with men and have overcome."'* (Genesis 32:27-28)

It was a moment that confirmed in him who he truly was. That day he knew he was no longer Jacob, the deceiver but Israel. This knowledge and understanding only came through a struggle, it came through his determination to hang onto God and refuse to let go. God knew that if Jacob was going to continue his journey, he had to leave behind the name 'deceiver' forever; it wasn't in keeping with the real

Jacob. Before he reconnected with Esau, God wanted to completely affirm in Jacob the discovery of who he was. The name 'Jacob' — the old identity all that went with it — was no longer fitting for this man of God.

Many people don't realise that God wants to be involved in their lives like this but I have realised that God is a great wrestling partner. Maybe right now you find yourself in a wrestle; it's a struggle, a situation that keeps knocking you down and won't let you go. Maybe you think it is the enemy and you have been praying for God to remove the wrestle from your world but have you considered the thought that God might have instigated it? This wrestle is not meant to harm you; this wrestle is going to make you become more 'you'.

Throughout your life you may have had names, labels and roles attached to you that have become part of your identity. This may be due to experiences you have been through, or a result of what other people have said to you. Many people take on labels given to them by others but they are fostering and feeding a wrong impression of who they are. They walk around carrying names like failure, rejected, useless; or they have a label that is one-dimensional like parent, wife or son. This ends up permeating their thinking and influences and limits the way they see their life. When we don't know who we are, it affects where we will go and what we are willing to attempt for God. Often, the only way to leave

your labels behind is to enter the wrestling ring and
answer the question, 'What is Your Name?'

Limping for life

Jacob never walked the same after his wrestle with God.
His hip was damaged and for the rest of his days he had
a limp. It was something that marked him. If you
wrestle with God, you need to know that you will also
be different when you come out on the other side.

Wrestling God on this identity journey will give you
something unique – your very own limp. It is a mark of
the experiences you have been through as an individual
on your journey. It is something that reminds you of the
price you paid to bring the real 'you' to the surface. You
can't copy the way someone limps after they have
wrestled with God, because their style is individual to
them.

Sometimes people may decide they want to straighten
out your limp because it makes them feel uncomfortable.
They have noticed how much it has changed you, that
there are relationships you have moved on from,
conversations you will no longer be part of and that you
have a new confidence in God that unsettles them from
their own comfort zone. We must resist the pressure to
conform and we must not hide our limps. Don't be afraid
to share your journey, as this will be the key to helping
others embark on their own.

Several times in my life, I have been aware that I have entered the wrestling ring and as much as I would rather not have to go through the struggle, I know it has become a unique part of who I am. My wrestle to become pregnant over five years was one such example. Steve and I had been told we could not conceive and were in the middle of getting help with fertility treatment. I was frustrated and annoyed with the situation. I remember one day going for a jog on the hills behind our house and talking to God about how I felt. I began venting my frustration saying, 'Why me, it's not fair, why can't I have a baby?' (All language I'm sure you'd never use with God, but I did.) The strangest thing happened to me that day. As I wept in frustration, my hip gave way and I began to limp. At first I thought I had pulled a muscle from running and as I hobbled along God said to me, 'Read about Jacob — he wrestled with God and it changed his walk forever — and this is about your limp'.

From that day forward, I never spoke to God again from a place of frustration about my infertility, because we made a deal together. I was going to get through the situation and at the end of it, he was going to give me something different to say than what came out of my mouth when I first entered the ring. I was getting a limp that was unique to me on my journey and would help others. I can honestly say that a new sense of compassion entered my life during that wrestle. I gained a new understanding of people's desperation when they faced similar difficulties and a real empathy for people's pain. What I learned has now become part of my gift to others. When I tell them about my journey, I am not just quoting someone else's life; I am giving away part of my identity and who I am. Are you willing to gain a limp for the sake of others? Jacob did and he was never the same again physically or spiritually.

Tour guide or traveller?

There are many Christians and leaders who have not got their own limp. They have no real scars. Paul said *"I bear on my body the marks of Jesus' (Galatians 6:17b)*, he didn't hide them but drew attention to them because they were part of his journey. They made him who he was. You can tell the difference between those who limp and those who don't. People who have no limp of their own are like tour guides who are giving out travel advice about destinations they have never been to. Their guidance can end up sounding hollow and can lack real depth, because it's not coming from their own journey; it's not coming from who they are but from what they know.

There is such a big difference between the description you will get about a place from someone who has only read about it and someone who has actually been there. When you have been somewhere, you have a completely different perspective on it. You can give great advice to people on where to go, on what to see and what pitfalls to look out for. You have a better idea of what going through this phase of their journey will do for them, because you have been there yourself. When you are sharing from a real, genuine experience, others can learn so much more from you. We all need to make sure that we don't settle for reading a guidebook when God wants us to experience the destination for ourselves.

I know I have been changed forever by the times I have wrestled with God. It has changed the way I speak and the way I see things. I know who I am and have the confidence to be myself. I can be confident in who I am, not in how well I perform or fulfil certain criteria. I know where my authority comes from but it all comes at a cost of being willing to walk differently.

Travelling companions

As I mentioned earlier in the book, although there will be moments of separation in your journey, they will help to connect you to the right people and relationships for your life.

Wherever you are on your journey, you will discover that God will connect you to others on a similar path. These connections are vital if we are to become all God wants us to be. When you begin to understand this, it changes the way you look at relationships, because you will want to look for people that God has purposefully put in your path. People who will embrace the real 'you', people who will see where you are going in life and encourage you to keep moving in the direction that is right for you.

On my journey, I have found that God has placed key people in my life at just the right time, who have become my travelling companions. These are not casual friendships but deep relationships that I know are a gift from God to my world. I have walked with some of these people for many years now and I know that the connection we have was not made by coincidence or chance, it was ordained by heaven. Travelling companions are special; they are rare and we need to learn how to recognise them in our world and invest in these valuable relationships that have such a crucial role in helping us on our journey of identity. So, having established that you must know who you are as a person, we will now take a more detailed look at the vital connections you need to make in order to move closer to being one hundred percent you.

'Men and women who **know** themselves are **no longer** fools; they **stand** on the threshold of the door of **wisdom.**'

Havelock Ellis

Chapter 7

Connected Living

If you look at people who are highly successful in leadership, business or other areas of life, they all have something in common. They have great people around them; people who accompany them on their journey and help turn their dreams into reality. Finding the right people to walk with is, therefore, a crucial part of successfully navigating your identity journey.

We often look at other people and assume that they have what it takes to make it through life alone because they are capable, confident riders who have no apparent 'stabilisers'. The reality is, no-one can complete their journey alone, we all need to live our lives connected to others. Jesus' journey teaches us how important this is. He chose twelve close travelling companions to be with him because being surrounded by crowds of people was insufficient. Jesus needed his team around him if he was to achieve all that was in his heart. They helped him spread the Gospel, they protected him, prayed with him and ministered alongside him. Jesus even turned to his disciples for help and support when he was facing the agony of the cross. He understood that living life connected and having the right people around him was a vital part of his journey. And if Jesus needed travelling companions, then I'm completely convinced that we can't do without them either.

If you were preparing to go on a long journey, I'm sure that you would think carefully about what to take with you. If you are anything like me, you would want to be organised ahead of time and make a list of all the essentials, so that everything you need is carefully packed before you set off. Choosing the right person is like selecting the right equipment for your journey. Having that person with you may be the equivalent of taking a map book with you because they have already travelled the same road on their own journey, so they have a good idea of what lies ahead. Or perhaps you need someone in your life who will act as a compass, who will speak up and encourage you to get back on track and keep moving in the right direction for your life if you start to drift off course.

Unfortunately, many of us set off without this vital equipment. Then, when we get lost or are facing difficulty, we send out an SOS emergency call, hoping someone will respond. The ones who do respond may not provide us with the kind of help we need for that particular crisis. They may simply react like the emergency services and pick you up off the floor but not stick around when you set off on the road again.

Solomon advised against this type of living when he spoke about living life connected. He said: *'Two are better than one, because they have a good return for their work: If one falls down, his friend can help him up. But pity the man who falls and has no-one to help him up,'* (Ecclesiastes 4:9-10) Yet, too many children of God try to cope alone, without ever experiencing the fulfilment that this kind of connected living brings.

Living life connected

When you start to truly connect with people at a deep relational level, it becomes possible for you to explore together all that God has put in you. On my personal journey, God has frequently placed key people in my path at just the right time who became my travelling companions. These were not casual friendships based on coincidence or chance but long-term connections that continue to hold destiny and purpose within them.

This kind of companionship is what God had in mind for us from the very beginning. After his creation, Adam was left in the Garden of Eden to tend to the animals and look after the plants but God knew that deep inside him was a yearning to have another person alongside him. Adam wasn't destitute or helpless but he was created by God with a need for companionship that had to be filled. So, *'The Lord God said, "It is not good for man to be alone. I will make a helper suitable for him,"'* (Genesis 2:18). The words God used here are very important. Adam didn't need a colleague, he wasn't longing for a servant or an associate to join his life to. Rather, the language God used was far more relational; he needed a helper and a companion and when Eve came along she was designed specifically for that purpose. Since that time, our innate need to build close relational connections hasn't changed; it is in our DNA and is the way we were designed. Without fulfilling this longing, we will never live our lives to one hundred percent of our potential. Because God calls us to be his House, his body and an army, these all require this kind of connected living to succeed.

Connected living is challenging but it helps you to discover who you really are and that is why you need it on this journey. I have found out so much more about myself through connecting my life to others than I would ever have discovered if I had stayed in isolation or just with surface relationships. I have had to be more honest and real as I joined my journey to others. My patience has had to increase along with my grace, love and forgiveness. Connected living has helped me become 'me'.

I discovered the value of connected living in a new way when I left home for the first time and went away to university. This period of time in my life was very challenging but also a very important one on my identity journey. Away from the comfort of my church, my Christian friends and home environment, I found myself suddenly having to express the real me. I deliberately chose to live with three girls who had a strong dislike for anything to do with God or church. They became great friends to me over those three years but it wasn't without its challenges. They confronted me about whether I really believed certain things and how committed I was as a Christian. Through them I learned to deal with differences of opinion and to embrace opposition.

I'm thrilled to say that one of my university friends is now a committed Believer; it seems that she also needed me in her journey. Several years later we were reunited and she shared how the time we had spent together had helped her discover more about her true identity. She went from being completely closed and shut off, to being open and embracing towards God. She's still the same crazy, vibrant, strong-willed girl that I was at University with, but now she has a 'God side'. It is this 'God side' that is being used to facilitate her God-given dreams, ideas and potential. It was always in her but she needed to be around other people to help it come out.

University helped me become a better me. I didn't just benefit educationally but it was also of great benefit to my personal development. Of course, you don't have to go to university to discover this, so don't panic. However, I do strongly urge you to get out more, to reach out and connect with different types of people. That's why I believe the House of God is so important. Without being planted in the House you can't possibly flourish because you are not connected. When I say planted I don't mean just attending; I mean deliberately getting involved, connecting with others and deciding to put yourself in.

Moses, David, Joshua and Solomon were all successful, strong leaders who had something in common. Every single one of them had close travelling companions who they connected their lives to. Just look at Moses, he was God's man to lead the children of Israel to freedom but without his companions he would not have been able to carry on. There was even a point in Moses' life when he was ready to give up because of the heavy burden of leading three million people. In the book of Numbers it says, *'The Lord said to Moses: 'Bring me seventy of Israel's elders who are known to you as officials and leaders among the people. Have them come to the Tent of Meeting, that they may stand there with you. I will come down and speak with you there, and I will take of the Spirit that is on you and put the Spirit on them. They will help you carry the burden of the people so that you will not have to carry it alone.' (Numbers 11:16-17)*

I love God's answer to Moses' problem! He didn't say, 'Don't worry Moses, I'll fix everything for you,' and he didn't give Moses more power to sort out the people. Instead, he told him to make more of the connections in his life. The solution to his problem was actually quite simple because the travelling companions he needed were already with him. The demand Moses placed on them by closely connecting himself to their lives meant they could start releasing the potential inside them. This in turn freed up Moses to get on with what God had called him to do. They needed each other on their journeys.

Finding your fit

Making the right God connections for your life has the added bonus of helping you see where you fit in. When you join your life to the right travelling companions, you will start to discover more about why God made you the way you are. Sometimes we can look at those who are journeying around us and think that we don't have much to offer them. Yet, Moses didn't need another Moses — he needed an Aaron and a Hur; David didn't need another David — he needed a Jonathan.

Until you find the right companions, your life can be difficult to make sense of. It is like being a misplaced piece of a jigsaw puzzle. One piece on its own appears to have little purpose; you can't tell by looking at it what it was designed to do or where it is supposed to fit. When you find the right relationships to connect with, it is like finding the missing pieces of the puzzle, because those people fit perfectly alongside your life. Their shape compliments your own and when you slot your life into place alongside theirs, the bigger picture of all you can achieve together through your lives becomes clear. You begin to understand why your life is a certain shape, why God has put you all together and what your joint purpose is. You realise why you are 'you'!

The relationship between Moses, Aaron, Hur and Joshua shows us what can happen when people find out how their lives fit together like this. We see this relational dynamic at work when they went into battle against the Amalekites:

'So Joshua fought the Amalekites as Moses had ordered, and Moses, Aaron and Hur went to the top of the hill. As long as Moses held up his hands, the Israelites were winning, but whenever he lowered his hands, the Amalekites were winning. When Moses, hands were tired, they took a stone and put it under him and he sat on it. Aaron and Hur held his hands up — one on one side, one on the other — so that his hands remained steady until sunset. So Joshua overcame the Amalekite army with the sword.'
(Exodus 17:10-13)

Moses, Joshua, Aaron and Hur had to find their fit together and play their part to win the battle. Moses was a strong leader, he didn't need 'stabilisers' in his life but he still needed companions who could do what he wasn't built to do. He was an old man who didn't have the strength and vigour of Joshua anymore. He needed Joshua to lead the army for him and two faithful encouragers called Aaron and Hur to hold his arms up for an entire day. By joining together, finding their fit and expressing who they were they each released the potential that was in their lives. Aaron and Hur were not in competition with Joshua, they weren't jealous that he got to wear the shining armour and be on the front line where he got all the victory and attention. Neither did they feel they were unfairly treated when Moses got to sit down but they just had to stand there all day.

I have thought a lot about why God did it this way. I mean, why didn't he let them win the battle without having to involve so many people and why did both of Moses' arms need raising? The more I look at this story, I can see it is such a beautiful illustration of how living life connected is not just a good idea but a God idea. It means that we all get to be part of the miracle and share each other's success. That day the victory was not just Joshua's or Moses', it also belonged to Aaron and Hur because they contributed by serving in the way that best suited who they were. I love that about God! He finds a way for you to be yourself and be part of the winning team. Life isn't about a few people having the most important roles; it's about each of us having an equally vital part to play by expressing what is inside us as we journey together.

This story about Moses, Aaron, Hur and Joshua has been a great encouragement to me on my journey because it has helped me understand more about my own identity and where I fit. From a young age I had a desire in my heart to serve in God's House alongside my Dad. I felt that my life and destiny was inextricably linked to his and knew that it was the right place for me to be. Some seven years ago, Paul led our church on an incredibly challenging journey as he re-invented who we were. He took us from being insular to being outward looking and from being cosy to being very uncomfortable, as we started to enlarge our circle of love and reach more people. At times, our journey was like going into battle as we fought against religion, people's mindsets and criticism. However, we refused to give up and established the God centred, purpose driven, people empowering culture that characterises our church today.

During that time, which we have since called 'Crossing Over', we chose to travel on a difficult path. There is no way I would have swapped places with Paul, because I could not have led the church through it. I didn't have the strength or the vision but I could see it in my heart and believed it was possible. So I stood alongside him, no matter what arrows were fired in our direction and I became like Aaron to my Moses. I supported his decisions; I protected the peace and fought for our freedom with him.

Many people still ask when Steve and I are going to plant our own church. I just smile at them because they really don't understand that I have already found my fit alongside Paul, which brings me into alignment with who I am and what God has created me to do. I am expressing the real me by holding up his arms and I am not looking for another job, because this is what I was built to do.

When you find your fit in this way, with the right people God has for your journey, you start to understand more about why God made you the way he did. When each of you starts to express and excel at being the real you, the combination of you all working together will bring results and great satisfaction, just like it did for Moses, Joshua, Aaron and Hur.

Chapter 8

Connection Criteria

Connected living, as I have explained it, requires us to take a look at our relationships with fresh eyes and start to see them from a God perspective. When was the last time that you took the time to think about why you are involved in certain relationships and what role they play in your life? We need to think more carefully and be more deliberate about who we connect our lives to. Have you got the right people alongside you for your journey, or are you getting held up and delayed by bad relational choices?

All your close relationships should be in your life by choice, they should be there for a purpose, not by accident or default. It may be that you have some people travelling with you that you need to separate from like Jacob did. It often takes courage to leave them behind and realign your life to the new connections that God has for you.

Choose your friends

When Esther, my youngest sister was growing up, she seemed to have the knack of finding a friend for every occasion. She had an ability to make friends with people who had things that she liked and often chose who she spent time with depending on what she fancied doing. So, she made friends with a girl whose parents had an indoor swimming pool at their house. Then, when the weather was bad, she could call her and go swimming. She had a friend with a quad bike for when the weather was nice enough to play outside and a friend with a horse for when she wanted to go riding. She also had a friend with a car so she could go shopping whenever she wanted. Esther had a friend for every occasion and although her criteria for choosing them were fairly materialistic, I've got to say she was smart for a twelve year old!

As Esther grew up and matured, her criteria for choosing her friends changed. She became more interested in who people were than what they had. Yet we can learn a lot from this, because many of us actually have no criteria established as a basis for selecting our relationships.

This question of the criteria we use is really crucial. We need to know who we are taking with us on our journey by asking the right questions before we set off. Sometimes we don't take the time to think this through properly and it can mean the difference between success and failure. You simply can't risk finding out that someone is not who you thought they were when you need them the most. Can you imagine what would have happened if Aaron and Hur had decided that they didn't want to hold Moses' arms up during the battle? Moses had to be completely sure that those close to him, the key players in his life, were with him one hundred percent. Otherwise, his entire journey and that of the three million people following him would have been put in jeopardy.

Asking questions and setting out clear criteria for choosing who you want to walk with, will help you distinguish between those who are your true journeying friends and others who are simply travellers you met along the way. We read in Amos, *'Do two people walk hand in hand if they aren't going to the same place?'* (3:3) Think about who you are holding hands with because they will affect where you end up. So, you have a responsibility to make sure that the relationships you are investing in will help keep you focused and moving in the right direction.

Before you form a new relational connection, stop and think about how it will grow your life, what its purpose is and whether it will help you discover more about who you really are. Is that new friend going to help you move on in your identity journey or try to make you be who they want you to be? Having this kind of deliberate approach will help you choose relationships that will be the most beneficial to your life.

If you don't deliberately make the right connections for your life and look for suitable travelling companions, then the enemy will happily fill your world with the wrong ones. David was someone who had first hand experience of how damaging it can be when you fail to make the right relational choices for your life. In 2 Samuel 11:1 we read that it was the time for *'Kings to go to war.'* Yet David didn't connect his life to the men he should have been leading, he didn't join his life to his army generals and fighting companions but chose to remain at home. Then, into the picture came Bathsheba; she was beautiful and alluring but she was not the right companion for the journey. The only reason this relationship ever became a valid option was because David had created a relational void in his life. By disconnecting his life from his men who were helping him achieve all that was in his heart, he had no-one to keep him on course. As a result, he ended up allowing his journey to be re-routed down paths he should never have been taking.

David pursued Bathsheba and connected his life to hers. She became pregnant, so he tried to cover up his wrong doing by bringing her husband, Uriah, home from the battlefield. He hoped that Uriah would sleep with his wife so no-one would ever know that the child she now carried was the result of an illicit liaison with the King. Uriah however, was living a connected life, he knew where he should be and that was fighting alongside his companions. He wouldn't even contemplate enjoying the comforts of being with his wife, when those he had chosen to join his life to were risking their lives on the battlefield.

When you are connected to the right people, like Uriah was, they will keep you focused firmly on your purpose. It becomes far more difficult for your journey to be derailed by the wrong relationships, because there isn't any space for them in your world. Your companions will help you to keep your momentum.

The story ended tragically. David arranged for Uriah to be killed so he could have Bathsheba for his wife. God was displeased with David for what he had done and it cost him the fulfilment of his dream to build God a House. This entire episode could have been avoided if David had kept his life connected to the right people. That one wrong relational choice for his life had far reaching consequences and shows us how vital it is for us to take the initiative in deciding who we connect our lives to.

So, let me ask: what criteria do you use to choose your friends? Have you ever taken the time to think through what qualities you are looking for in a person? I know we can never know everything there is to know about a person in advance, but there is a great deal we can learn by asking a few simple questions and following our God-given instinct.

To help answer these questions I want to look at some of the great travelling companions in God's Word, people like David and Jonathan, Ruth and Naomi, and Esther and Mordecai. We can learn so much from the connection criteria they used to help them make wise relational choices as they selected companions who had a crucial part to play in the success of their journeys.

Chapter 9

Secure Companions

First of all, I want to look at the life of Jonathan. He was on his own identity journey and had to make a difficult choice about who to connect his life to. Often there is a great amount of emphasis placed on the relationship between David and Saul and we forget that it was Jonathan who was caught in the crossfire between them. He had to decide between being loyal to his dad or following the pull of his heart towards David, who was ultimately his rival for the throne. He had to choose between the comfort of a palace lifestyle or the life of a fugitive. Jonathan was torn between staying attached to the 'stabilisers' of his dad's army or the scariness of disconnecting his life from it and going it alone. He had to make some tough decisions but each decision brought him closer to who he was and helped him express his true identity. He wasn't going to be defined by the label of being the king's son and he refused to live a life within the boundaries and limitations set for him by other people.

Yet, why did Jonathan choose David as his travelling companion, rather than Saul? I believe that Jonathan saw something in David that was a high priority on his list of connection criteria. It was present in David but absent from Saul's life — that criteria was security.

It says in 1 Samuel 18 that *'After David had finished talking with Saul, Jonathan became one in spirit with David, and he loved him as himself. From that day Saul kept David with him and did not let him return to his father's house. And Jonathan made a covenant with David because he loved him as himself. Jonathan took off the robe he was wearing and gave it to David, along with his tunic, and even his sword, his bow and his belt.' (1-4)*

I've often wondered why Jonathan decided to risk everything he had known and grown up with, just on the basis of overhearing one conversation. When he heard David, the secure young shepherd speaking with Saul the insecure King, his heart leapt within him. He listened to Saul's insecurity, his confusion and defensiveness and compared it to David's security, calmness and confidence. He recognised the clear, distinct sound of security that came from David's life and knew in his heart that he needed him on his journey.

Jonathan was also secure in who he was. He didn't spend weeks moping around the palace trying to figure out what to do and deciding whether he could live without his royal status and privileges. He saw no glory in being King, because that role was not in keeping with who he was. He just felt a deep and instant conviction about connecting his life to David.

A secure life is the sign of a well journeyed person who understands their identity. They have discovered who they really are and are confident to be themselves. Many people try to fake their security, or get it by borrowing someone else's but it's not something that they can sustain for long. Soon, insecurity starts to reveal itself. It shows itself in the boss who takes all the credit for his employee's great idea. It shows itself in the person who can't celebrate the success of their friend and it shows itself in the singer who gets a big attitude when someone else on the worship team is asked to do the solo this week. Insecurity shows up in many different guises but its results are the same; it damages lives and can be very destructive.

Saul is a great example of what can happen if you try to fake your security. The problems began on the day he was crowned King as we read, *'Finally Saul son of Kish was chosen. But when they looked for him he was not to be found. So they inquired of the Lord further, "Has the man come here yet?" And the Lord said, "Yes, he has hidden himself among the baggage."'* (1 Samuel 10:21b-22)

You would expect the future King to be strong and brave but Saul's behaviour that day revealed the insecurity in his heart. You can understand why he felt that way; he was plucked from obscurity and made King because he looked the part and must have had so many unresolved issues in his heart about his true identity. It's one thing to grow up in a royal court, with an understanding of who you are being forged within you from a young age but a completely different matter to be a 'nobody' one day and to be promoted to the top job in the land the next. This rapid change in his status did not give him the time to make his own identity journey and he was left feeling inadequate and insecure.

Saul's behaviour that day should have rung warning bells and alerted people to who he really was but it didn't. Instead, as his insecurity began to show through, he surrounded himself with companions who stabilised him and stroked his fragile ego and this had disastrous results for his own life and the lives of the people he led.

Secure to release

Jonathan was the complete opposite of his father because he wasn't interested in power, status or control; he was secure enough to release people. He had every reason to hold David back but instead, he recognised who David was and did everything he could to help him reach his destiny. He chose to be an encourager and a protector to David and all that he carried in his life. It was only his own secure heart that made this possible. Secure people, like Jonathan, in turn release others to express their true identities. Their encouragement and belief in you acts as a springboard that helps you take giant leaps in the direction you are travelling. Instead of feeling the need to compete, they let their own lives, gifts and callings compliment yours, because they understand how your respective lives are designed to fit together. Secure people are people releasers by nature. They love to see other people soar in life; they empower and encourage others to go for their dreams and want to help them get to their destination. That is why I am unwilling to compromise on the criteria of security when I choose my travelling companions.

Jesus is our ultimate role model for seeing what a life committed to being a people releaser looks like. He believed in the potential of those around him and encouraged them to keep stretching and growing their lives. He would even let them tackle situations that he already knew how to handle, just to try and help them make progress on their own identity journeys. Jesus even said to his disciples, *'I tell you the truth, anyone who has faith in me will do what I have been doing. He will do even greater things than these.' (John 14:12)*
Only a secure person can encourage others to go beyond where they have been and achieve more than they did. We need to have the same approach to the people whose lives we influence and also look for people who can add this kind of empowerment to our own journey.

When people have this kind of security, walking with them becomes a very liberating experience. In my own journey I have chosen to do life with people who are committed to empowering others and being 'people empowering' is one of the foundations we have built into our church. Having an empowering culture allows people to excel in their areas of gift and calling, it gives them the space to grow big lives and dream big dreams. For many people this is not the case, as they are journeying with 'Saul', who refuses to empower those around him because he fears losing his position and influence to the 'David' they represent. Saul's insecurity keeps their real identity locked up. We need to realise that we share in the success of those we choose to walk with. By aligning your life with David, you get to celebrate his success, just as Jonathan shared each one of David's victories because they were of one heart.

Security brings stability

There is a big difference between living a life with 'stabilisers' and living a stable life. A 'stabilised life' is one that has to be propped upright by external supports, but a 'stable life' is one that has the momentum and skill to stay balanced without them. Stable people have learned to ride on all kinds of terrain; they have journeyed far enough to know how to keep upright. Stability is a characteristic of a secure life and it is a quality that will enhance your own journey.

As I mentioned in the previous chapter, there are many vital pieces of equipment you would want to take with you on a journey. I would imagine that anyone wanting to find their way would choose to take a compass with them. A stable companion is like having a compass. The direction it gives you does not change. No matter what the weather is like, or how steep the road you are walking on becomes, it never moves. North is always going to be true north. This gives you confidence to keep walking because you can rely on the reading.

Stable people stay calm when you are facing difficulties, they don't suddenly start wobbling and fall over. Jonathan helped bring stability to parts of David's journey. There was one particular time when David was in turmoil, because Saul was trying to kill him and he had to flee for his life. Jonathan stayed right by his side throughout; he didn't back out, he didn't leave him, but committed to help him saying, *'Whatever you want me to do, I'll do for you,' (1 Sam 20:4)*. He was risking his own life by going against his father, and Jonathan knew what Saul was capable of. He had grown up with this insecure man, seeing the fits of rage and jealousy that consumed him but Jonathan was secure, he was stable and his actions did not depend on circumstances.

An insecure person has the opposite response, they are changeable in their emotions and they are not consistent in their reactions to situations. It's like having a compass that will change its settings from north to south depending on the weather, or will stop working randomly for no reason and with no warning. Taking this kind of person with you will slow you down and they will confuse you about the direction you are supposed to take. Insecure people will make you lose momentum as you have to waste valuable time trying to work out where they are at, instead of concentrating on the challenges that lie ahead.

Security should always be high on our list of criteria for choosing our relationships. Having people like Jonathan in your life will be a valuable support on your journey. They bring empowerment to your life; they will release and encourage you to go for your dreams and will be a stabilising influence when you face your greatest times of testing and challenge. They will help get the real you out; they won't feel threatened by you or try to control you because they are secure in who they are.

In complete contrast to this, insecurity will take you to a place you were never supposed to go. Jonathan, the secure companion, that courageous young man who had his whole life ahead of him, died with his father, fighting a battle they should never have been in. It was yet another misguided detour from Saul's intended route that his insecurity took him on and it cost him his life. This shows how important a priority having secure companions is, if we want to get the most from our journey and reach our final destination.

Chapter 10

Long Distance Companions

Of all the different people you connect with on your journey, some relationships will only be seasonal. You will share the same route and walk together for a while but then the time will come for you to go your separate ways. When you are young, you tend to think that all your friendships will be life-long but as you grow and mature, you see them differently. You realise that in order to make some friendships last for the long haul, you will have to put in far more energy and commitment than was needed before. In order to build a great life, you have to get some permanence relationally, you need to connect your life to long distance travelling companions and not rely on the seasonal ones.

With longevity comes intimacy. Long distance companions get to see the real you, they will share your successes and see your failures. They will be with you in times of laughter and times of tears. For some people this is a frightening thought; they simply don't want to let anyone see who they really are. To make sure their true identity is never discovered by their friends, they uncouple their lives from people early on in the journey.

I once counselled a young lady like this who came to our church. She was a great girl who had a bright, lively personality and soon made lots of friends. After a while a pattern developed in her life and every few months she would swap friends. She couldn't journey with anyone long-term and this became evident throughout every area of her life; in friendships, in her job, in the way she served at church and with romantic attachments. As we talked, she admitted that she didn't want people to truly know who she was. She just wanted them to think she was a great, fun girl to be around. Once they wanted to know her on a deeper level, she would back off for fear of having to give away more about her true identity. She didn't want them to see her insecurities or fears. This girl was short-circuiting all her relational connections on purpose because she didn't know how to handle long distance companions.

Many people make this mistake and stay in 'short sprint' relationships so they can hide their faults and weaknesses. That's why marriage can seem such a scary experience for some people, because it is a commitment to journey for life with your partner. Yet we all need long distance friends, because they are the people who see us for who we really are and still love us for being our true selves.

On my journey, I have discovered the benefits of having 'long distance friends' on my list of criteria. These are people who are crazy enough to want to link themselves with me for life! We have a special connection because our identities and destinies are inextricably linked by God's design. I can't shake them off and they can't shake me off.

The value of having a long distance friend is best seen in the lives of two travelling companions called Ruth and Naomi. At the time I don't think Naomi was looking for a long distance companion but God knew she needed one. We find her widowed and destitute, having lost her husband and two sons. All she had left in the world were her two daughters-in-law, Ruth and Orpah, who were Moabites. Naomi decided it was time for her to return to her homeland of Judah and she gave them the choice of whether to accompany her or stay with their own people. Faced with this option Ruth said, *'Don't urge me to leave you or to turn back from you. Where you go I will go, and where you stay I will stay. Your people will be my people and your God my God. Where you die I will die, and there I will be buried. May the Lord deal with me, be it ever so severely, if anything but death separates you and me.'* *(Ruth 1:16-17)*

Sometimes, it's only when a particular situation forces you to make a choice that this type of companion comes to your attention. It's easy to make the mistake of thinking that the people who are in your world now will always be there but I have travelled through enough storms to know the reality is very different. Many of our companions in life are not built for the long haul.

In an athletics team there are many different runners who each excel at particular distances. You have those who love to sprint in the one hundred or two hundred metres, the middle distance runners who can run a couple of kilometres before they tire and then there are the long distance athletes, the marathon runners who can go for twenty-six miles without stopping. They each have the determination to make the distance and keep going until they have completed their race. My point here is that you and I need to make sure that we know what type of distance each of our travelling companions can go. Each has a part to play on your journey but those who can go the long distance with you will be the ones who help you the most when it comes to discovering more about your own identity. They will stay beside you through the storm and after the storm — they are priceless.

So how can we find out who our long distance friends are? Maybe you already have some or maybe you still need to find them. Ruth was already alongside Naomi, and it's possible that there is someone like her in your world but you haven't discovered their true identity yet. Naomi had no way of distinguishing between Ruth and Orpah until she told them of her intention to go back to Judah. Sometimes it will take a challenging situation to show you the true nature of some of your relationships.

In many ways, you don't choose your long distance friends, they choose you. It's both special and rare for someone to make this kind of commitment to another person and it is not something that you can coerce or force. Naomi didn't ask for that level of loyalty from Ruth, it tumbled out of her heart. Persuasion will not make someone willing to stay with you for the long haul. The commitment has to come from their own heart and be given freely. We can learn much from how Naomi handled the situation. She had clearly mapped out her own journey and allowed the girls to choose whether they could make the distance. It was this that showed her the difference between Orpah and Ruth. By releasing people to make a choice you will soon discover who wants to stay with you.

Run your race

Orpah is someone who I feel is often misunderstood in this story. People think she had a bad heart or was selfish when compared to Ruth, because she chose to separate from Naomi. I don't believe this. Orpah loved her mother-in-law dearly. It even says that when they parted, '*they wept again. Then Orpah kissed her mother-in-law good-bye but Ruth clung to her,' (Ruth 1:14)* These two women expressed deep concern and care towards each other and it was a real wrench to Orpah's heart when she had to leave. This decision was about Orpah being true to who she was, not about any emotional attachment she felt towards her mother-in-law. She had to be honest about her true identity because she knew that she could not complete the journey that lay ahead. It was a distance that she was not built to run, she could never be like Ruth and by letting Naomi know that, she gave her a gift.

It says in Hebrews that we should, *'run with perseverance the race marked out for us,' (12:1c)* but sometimes we can try to make other people compete in the wrong race. The race they are called to run may not be the same one you have been in training for. If someone is only designed to walk with you for two kilometres, they will not have the stamina or the conviction to keep going for another ten. Instead of being an encouragement and help, they will soon start to complain about how sore their feet are and drive you crazy asking how much further they have to go!

Orpah was destined for a different race to Naomi and Ruth; it was a race that would take her back to her family in Moab, not to Judah. She would not have had the pace or the will to complete the race that was marked out for them.

Ruth was different to Orpah; she knew that her identity was only going to be found by staying with Naomi. The long journey didn't deter her because she had a deep conviction in her heart that this was the right relational connection for her life. She had no guarantees of what would happen and she didn't have a place to stay or the promise of another husband or family. Although the rest of her circumstances were unclear, Ruth clung to Naomi because that was one thing she was totally convinced about and it was enough to make her go on the journey.

On my own journey I have been through times when I was unsure what to say or do next. I am unclear about many things but the one thing I am certain about is that my life is connected to the right people, so I stay close to them. It's like following a convoy in the dark. Steve and I once went to a New Years celebration in the Lake District and we had no idea where we were going. Our friends who had the map were in the car in front and wc were following them. We came to a point in the journey when it was snowing heavily, the wind was howling and we were surrounded by dense fog. We even lost the signal on our mobile phone because we were in the middle of nowhere. All we could do was stay as close as possible to the dim fog lamps we could see on the car ahead and keep going. Eventually we regained some clarity to our situation as the fog cleared and we arrived safely at our destination.

Sometimes, when everything else in your life is unclear, you just need to know who Naomi is in your world and stay close. That's what Ruth did and it brought Boaz into her world, who was to be another of her long distance friends. This time, it was Boaz who was the pursuer; he sought Ruth out and was determined to connect his life to hers by making her his wife.

Ruth found out who she truly was by accompanying Naomi on her journey. It ultimately brought her to Boaz, her destiny and the fulfilment of her desire to have a family. Yet their relationship was mutually beneficial, because Naomi also discovered a new sense of her own identity. I love the last few verses in Ruth that describe what happened when Ruth's child was born. It says, *'The town women said to Naomi, "Blessed be God! He didn't leave you without family to carry on your life. May this baby grow up to be famous in Israel! He'll make you young again! He'll take care of you in old age. And this daughter-in-law who has brought him into the world and loves you so much, why, she's worth more to you than seven sons!" Naomi took the baby and held him in her arms, cuddling him, cooing over him, waiting on him hand and foot.' (Ruth 4:14-16 The Message)*

This was Ruth's baby, so why did the women say he was Naomi's son? It was because their relational connection was so deep that everyone saw this child as also being Naomi's family; he was God's blessing to her life as well as Ruth's. It was also her destiny to have a family and not to be left alone. This baby was a shared joy and a shared fulfilment of their hopes and dreams. When they set off on their journey to Judah, neither of them knew how significant their connection to each other would be. Ruth had no idea what would happen on the way but her obedience and her willingness to follow her instinct and stay with Naomi led both of them towards their destinies.

So, when you are choosing your travelling companions, make sure that you include 'long distance friends' on your list of criteria. They are the type of people you just cannot shake off, whatever you say to them to try and deter them. You can tell them how hard the journey is, you can tell them what it might cost but it makes no difference. They are coming with you, like it or not, because they know their destiny and purpose is inextricably linked to yours and they were built with the stamina to go the distance you need to travel together.

You will find that there are only a few people who will be a Ruth or a Jonathan to you; they are rare and you may even only find them once in your entire life. Henry Adams once wrote, *'One friend in a life-time is much, two are many, three are hardly possible.'* Real friendships, especially long distance ones like this are rare, so, when you find them, you should treasure them and enjoy their company as you travel through life together.

Chapter 11

Honest Companions

No matter how strong we feel we are, or how much we have God's favour and blessing on our lives, we still need people in our world who will speak the truth on our journey; those who will speak up to prevent us from taking a wrong turn. Sometimes we think that God will be the one to direct us and correct us but often he does it through other people. We need to choose travelling companions, who are honest and open enough to bring correction to our lives when necessary.

It may sound like a complete contradiction but friendship is supposed to wound! Some of the most valuable relationships in your life will be the ones where people will tell you the truth about yourself, even when it hurts. Proverbs 27:6 says, *'Wounds from a friend can be trusted, but an enemy multiplies kisses.'* Although it doesn't sound like a desirable criterion to have on your list, wounding and friendship are supposed to go hand in hand.

Without companions who correct us, we risk becoming reckless, irresponsible travellers, because we are not living an accountable journey. If a certain area of your life is spoiling your walk, then you need people who love you enough to challenge you about it. We need to build friendships where we can be honest with each other. If you want to keep growing and progressing on your journey, then you need to be willing to welcome people into your life who will potentially wound you.

David was a strong character. He was known for both his leadership ability and his prowess on the battlefield. Yet, he needed equally strong, courageous people around him who were not afraid to speak up. David discovered the value of having an honest companion, called Joab, when he faced one particularly difficult situation. Joab stepped forward at a time when David's journey was about to be derailed by compromise, because of an unwise relational connection he had to his son Absalom. David had a deep attachment to his son but his love was not reciprocated. Absalom deceived, cheated and lied to his father and plotted to overthrow him. After four years of subversion and animosity, Joab and his men caught and killed Absalom and sent word of his demise to the palace.

They expected this news to be welcomed. After all, Absalom had brought it on himself through his disloyalty and betrayal, and David had been on the run from him. Instead, however, David was overcome by grief. He was so consumed by Absalom's death that he forgot about the men who had risked their lives on the battlefield to protect him and his family from Absalom. He ignored the sacrifice they had made for him and what should have been a day spent celebrating their victory, became one of uneasy tension and mourning, as news of the King's reaction spread.

At this point, Joab the honest companion stepped in. It was not the norm for a military chief to correct the King but David and Joab were long distance friends. They had journeyed through many battles together and Joab would not stand back and watch David make such a grave mistake. Joab knew the real David, he could clearly see that his behaviour was out of step with his true identity — so he told the King exactly what he thought and did not hold back.

'Then Joab went to the house of the king and said, "Today you have humiliated all your men, who have just saved your life and the lives of your sons and daughters and the lives of your wives and concubines. You love those who hate you and hate those who love you. You have made it clear today that the commanders and their men mean nothing to you. I see that you would be pleased if Absalom were alive today and all of us were dead. Now go out and encourage your men. I swear by the Lord that if you don't go out, not a man will be left with you by nightfall. This will be worse for you than all the calamities that have come upon you from your youth till now."' (2 Samuel 19:5 -7)

If Joab had not been willing to correct David, he would have lost the respect and support of his entire army that day. Joab was an honest companion who saw past David's behaviour and emotional turmoil; he spoke truth into his life, bringing a fresh perspective and clarity to the situation. He was prepared to wound his friend, who was already feeling tender, in order to save him from a far worse fate. Joab knew that if David didn't change his attitude, he would also lose his faithful travelling companions who loved him.

Proverbs 14:25 says, *'A truthful witness saves lives, but a false witness is deceitful.'* We all need people like Joab who will be that truthful witness to us. They are the companions who will make a massive difference in your world by encouraging you to raise your game. 'Joabs' aren't satisfied with you doing a good job if they know there is more in your life than that. They will always push you, challenge you and cajole you to go higher and to keep stepping up in life from average to excellence. You can trust that if an honest companion brings a measure of pain to your life, it is because you stand to gain something through it. It is pain for a purpose.

Pruning on purpose

Jesus said, *'I am the true vine, and my Father is the gardener. He cuts off every branch in me that bears no fruit, while every branch that does bear fruit he prunes so that it will be even more fruitful,' (John 15:1-2)* We all have things in our lives that need pruning away if we want to bear fruit. So, if you want to have a fruitful life, you need people in your world who will not hesitate to use the pruning shears. You must accept that pruning can often be a painful process, but still be willing to give permission to those you trust to chop off any branches that are stunting your personal growth.

If you don't allow your life to be constantly pruned, you will start to struggle on your identity journey. The branches that should have been cut off will slow you down and you will end up being delayed and held up as you try to continue on your journey with branches you should have lost a long time ago. A life that is never pruned will eventually come to a standstill because the extra 'branches' growing from your life will become a hindrance. You will end up carrying so much extra weight that it will be a struggle to keep going. Remember, the aim of your identity journey is to discover who you really are but as long as you allow things to grow in your life that shouldn't be there, you are never going to reach your full potential.

If you observe a lack of fruit in the lives of some people around you, then maybe it is because they have not chosen honest travelling companions; ones who are willing to wound them. They have nobody to come alongside them with pruning shears and warn them that unless they change their negative outlook, their journey will be delayed. We have to remember that ultimately fruitfulness comes from pruning. So, if you want your life to produce a bumper crop of fruit, you need to invite pruning and wounding friends to journey with you.

Hurt that helps

I remember an occasion when I was given some hurt that helped. At the time I didn't see it as helpful, I just remember feeling wounded but the wound served a purpose. It happened several years ago when Steve and I went to see a specialist because we were struggling to have children. We discussed the problems we were having in conceiving and he assessed whether or not we should try fertility treatment. At first I thought he was such a fantastic and understanding doctor but then he turned to me and said, 'Mrs Gambill, if you don't mind me saying, you're overweight!' He suddenly went down in my estimation and I thought, 'I don't like you anymore! We were getting along very well but now you're telling me I'm fat!' My whole demeanour changed and although I'd been nodding in agreement with everything he said, now I couldn't wait to get out of the place because I was so offended. I thought, 'How dare you!'

Once I had calmed down and got over my indignation and embarrassment, I thought about what had been said. I had to admit, the doctor was right. So, I started to diet and lost a lot of weight because he had the guts to confront me. I laugh about it now because I know he didn't say it to hurt me; he said it to help me. He knew that by losing some weight, medically I would stand more chance of having a baby.

We even went back to see him and introduced him to our daughter, Hope Cherish, and I personally thanked him for his honesty. I said, 'I want to thank you for telling me I was overweight, because I needed to hear that, and no-one else dared to be that honest with me for fear of offending me. I'm so glad you were honest because now I feel so much healthier.' He looked surprised and said, 'Oh, you're welcome'. I don't think he was used to being thanked for that type of advice!

That specialist didn't have a personal vendetta against me. He was just trying to be helpful, and I had to decide whether to accept his help or ignore his advice, because he upset me. Sadly, many Christians choose the latter. Too often I have sat with people who are facing difficulties in life and thought, 'If only you would just listen to the voices in your world who are trying to help you, you could have such a great life. You could build a better future; you could have a much better marriage and a better relationship with your kids.' Often though, they can't get past the fact that people are wounding them. We must realise that we need honest friends and carefully decide who should speak into our lives like this. If it is from one of your trusted travelling companions, who you know has your best interests at heart, then although it may hurt at the time, maybe it's hurt that can help.

As we saw in a previous chapter, Saul was someone who was sadly lacking in honest companions. He had no-one to confront his insecurity, jealousy and rage and the lack of correction in his life eventually contributed to his destruction. As I mentioned earlier in this chapter, Proverbs 27:6 says, *'Wounds from a friend can be trusted, but an enemy multiplies kisses,'* and that is exactly what his companions did to him through their lack of honesty. Friends like this are not going to help you. Their flattery may make you feel better but you need friends who go beyond your feelings; friends who are committed to your long-term health and the success of your journey. I believe Saul's life could have had a happier ending if there had been someone like Joab in his inner circle who was willing to speak up.

So when you are looking for journeying friends, make sure that you always include honest people who will be faithful enough to wound you, because those are the ones you can trust. The truth they speak into your life will help keep you heading in the right direction. It says in Proverbs, *'Whoever loves discipline loves knowledge, but he who hates correction is stupid,'* *(Proverbs 12:1).* This means that anyone who refuses to embrace wounding friendships is only hurting themself. So you must find honest companions to walk with and be accountable to them for the way you live. Connect your life to people who love you and believe in you enough to speak the truth and help shape the real you.

Wise companions

Honesty goes hand in hand with wisdom. When you are an honest companion, you bring wisdom into the world of your friends because you are willing to share your journey. This is wisdom that we all need on our travels; a practical, well-worn and often hard-earned wisdom that helps us negotiate our personal journey more successfully.

It says in Proverbs 13:20, '*He who walks with the wise grows wise, but a companion of fools suffers harm*'. This highlights how important it is not only to get wisdom but to walk with wise people and to deliberately choose to travel with them. Wise friends are something you will not do well without!

Solomon was the wisest man who ever lived. He understood that having wisdom was worth more than anything else he could possess and valued it more than riches. He wrote in Proverbs, '*wisdom is more precious than rubies, and nothing you desire can compare with her,*' (*Proverbs 8:11*). We really need to desire wisdom for our journey. When you desire something, you don't have a passive attitude towards it. You actively seek it out because you know you need it. Wisdom is worth making the effort to gain, because embracing it will both protect you and help you find the right route for your journey.

Well-journeyed friends

There are plenty of people in the world who are willing to give you their advice but that doesn't mean they are wise, or will actually help you grow. The wisdom that has most benefited my life has often not seemed to be deep or particularly profound at first sight. It has been very down-to-earth and practical, with 'how to' explanations from others who have shared honestly from their own journey.

David understood the value of practical wisdom and advice from more experienced people and he became the source of it to his son Solomon. He made detailed preparations to help Solomon build the temple because he wanted him to benefit from all he had learned on his life-long journey. David said to the whole assembly on several occasions, *'My son Solomon, the one whom God has chosen, is young and inexperienced.' (1 Chronicles 29:1a)*

This was not belittling Solomon or making fun of him, he was simply aware of the areas his son needed the most help with. Solomon had the strength and vigour of youth; he was full of passion and energy but that wasn't enough. David knew Solomon needed wise companions around him, who had already travelled a long way on their own journeys, from whom he could learn. So, he made sure that he played his part in that process by passing on the wisdom he had to Solomon about how to build God's House the right way. David refused to leave it to chance but took responsibility for equipping him with everything he needed to be successful on his journey.

Sadly, some people are unwilling to share their experiences with those around them, because it means admitting the mistakes they have made; it means being real about who they really are. Wisdom is something we all need to help us on our way and when others are willing to let us learn what they have gleaned from their journeys, it is priceless.

Esther was someone else who benefited from having a well-journeyed friend in her life. He was called Mordecai. A decree had been sent out by her husband, King Xerxes, ordering the execution of all Jews in Persia on a certain date. Mordecai was convinced that Queen Esther, who was a Jewess, could stop it from happening. He urged her to act on behalf of her people but she was, understandably, fearful of losing her life. We read: *'When Esther's words were reported to Mordecai, he sent back this answer: "Do not think that because you are in the king's house you alone of all the Jews will escape. For if you remain silent at this time, relief and deliverance for the Jews will arise from another place, but you and your father's family will perish. And who knows but that you have come to royal position for such a time as this?"' (Esther 4:12-14)*

Mordecai's wisdom helped Esther understand the context of her life. He explained that she was facing a destiny-defining moment. It's at times like these that you need wise companions with you on the journey. They are less fearful than you are, because they have journeyed further. Consequently, they bring a wisdom that steadies you and keeps you on course — just like Mordecai did for Esther that day. They will help you keep moving in the right direction, even when you feel like turning back.

When looking for companions, I think that we naturally gravitate towards people who are like us. We are attracted to those who have similar interests or experiences in life but if you want to connect your life to the wisdom you need for your journey, you may have to look further a field. Look for people who have already travelled further than you; seek out well-journeyed friends, who understand the challenges you face and know how to successfully negotiate a way through the difficult terrain on the road ahead. They have this wealth of knowledge because they have already travelled the road. They have lived through similar experiences to those you are facing and are willing to let you benefit from the lessons they have learned. Their lives contain valuable wisdom that will help you on your way.

A house of wisdom

The first place we should look for these wise companions is in the House of God. At the start of this book, I mentioned how I love the diversity of God's

House and one reason for this is because I believe this incredible mixture of people can add a great deal to your journey. God's House is filled with people who are further along the path that you may just have started on and therefore they are able to add wisdom to your journey, both spiritually and practically.

Titus chapter 2 describes something of how God's House should be a place where people exchange their travelling wisdom. We read:

'Teach the older men to be temperate, worthy of respect, self-controlled, and sound in faith, in love and in endurance. Likewise, teach the older women to be reverent in the way they live, not to be slanderers or addicted to much wine, but to teach what is good. Then they can train the younger women to love their husbands and children, to be self-controlled and pure, to be busy at home, to be kind, and to be subject to their husbands, so that no one will malign the word of God. Similarly, encourage the young men to be self-controlled'. (Titus 2:2-6)

These verses describe an exchange of wisdom that was going on, not only between friends but also between generations. It illustrates how those further on in their journey can help those coming along behind. This exchange is what should be happening naturally in God's House. If you need to learn how to do something, then it makes complete sense for you to seek advice from someone who has already succeeded.

When I got married I needed some new travelling companions in addition to those I had travelled with when I was single. My new companions needed to be people who had successfully travelled along the road Steve and I were starting out on. I soon learned that there was little point in listening to people who could quote the right verses to do with marriage but had never put those truths into practice! My well-travelled single friends were unable to help me avoid making mistakes on a road they had never travelled. We needed to be alongside travellers who had been this way before, learn from their success and avoid making the same poor choices they had made. Their wisdom was invaluable to us. Now, years later we find ourselves helping other newly married couples on their journey. That is how God intended it to be, with those who have travelled further in certain areas of life helping those who are just beginning.

This approach to finding wise companions applies to every area of life. Sometimes in our church context, we can think that 'wisdom' is all about spiritual matters but the truth is, you need wisdom about all kinds of things if you want to excel in life. You may need wisdom about how to manage your finances, or a career choice, or about how to raise a great family. There are many life skills that you need to grow and develop in, if you want your journey to be a success. I believe that much of the wisdom we need for life and for our journey should be found in the House of God. Wise king Solomon, who had benefited from his wise father and good companions said, *'You use steel to sharpen steel, and one friend sharpens another'* *(Proverbs 27:17 The Message).* We need to check that our companions have travelled far enough on their own journeys to help us out at the stage we are at. So, before you ask someone for advice, think about whether they are someone who can truly sharpen your life.

George Eliot summed up the value of having honest and wise travelling companions as follows: *'Oh, the comfort, the inexpressible comfort of feeling safe with a person: having neither to weigh thoughts nor measure words, but to pour them out. Just as they are – chaff and grain together, knowing that a faithful hand will take and sift them, keep what is worth keeping, and then with the breath of kindness, blow the rest away.'*

Enjoy the journey

Before we move on to the last section of this book, I want to highlight one final criterion we should use when choosing our companions. We all need friends who are fun; people who will help you to enjoy the journey. Proverbs 17:22 says, *'A cheerful heart is good medicine, but a crushed spirit dries up the bones.'* Being around cheerful people is good for you. Their cheer helps you enjoy the journey and gets you through difficult or challenging times.

When you think about the great friendships we have looked at in earlier chapters, you can see that enjoyment was a common theme running through them all. David enjoyed Jonathan's company; they had a great friendship filled with fun, as well as adventure and danger. Ruth enjoyed Naomi's company and together they helped each other through a very difficult time but no doubt, had many a laugh along the way. Jesus enjoyed himself. He loved to socialise with people and enjoyed being with his disciples, for the most part. They made him laugh and they had fun on their travels together. I believe that one of the reasons Jesus is described as being a friend to many was because he was such good fun. People enjoyed themselves when they were with him.

When you compare these friendships to the joyless companions that Job shared his life with, you can see how important it is to have the right people around you. Instead of being medicine to his heart by having a cheerful spirit, they became like poison to his soul. If it wasn't for Job's own strength of character and faith in God, he would never have got through those times.

Some Christians talk much about the 'joy of the Lord' but rarely seem to express it. Real joy is not something you can hide away in your heart, it is full of life; it is something that will make you smile. Joy is infectious and will spread to those your life touches. It says in Nehemiah 8:10c that *'the joy of the Lord is your strength.'* Joy and strength are partners; they go together. This journey of discovery you are on, finding out who you really are and what you were created to do, requires strength.

Having joy is fuel for your journey and keeps you going during the times when you want to give up. So, if you are feeling weak today, then maybe you don't need more prayer, direction or even more help; you need more joy. Joy can come in many ways, but how better than through fun-loving, joy-bringing friends.

Enjoy or endure

Every step of the journey is to be enjoyed but some have turned it into an endurance course. The brother of the prodigal son made this mistake. He was enduring his journey as he slaved away working hard, waiting for the day when he would finally receive a big pay-out from his inheritance. He became furious when his father threw a party on his younger brother's return home from squandering his share of their family's wealth. So, he refused to join in the celebrations. His father said, '*My son, you are always with me, and everything I have is yours. But we had to celebrate and be glad, because this brother of yours was dead but now he is alive again; he was lost and is found.*' (*Luke 15:31-32*)

The older brother had made the mistake of failing to enjoy his journey; everything he could have wished for was already around him and there to be enjoyed. He needed to change his perspective and instead of thinking joy would come one day in the future, he needed to enjoy the day he was in.

Having two young children has reminded me, very practically, about how important it is to enjoy your journey. We try to make every journey we take as a family as much fun as the final destination. In that way, we enjoy our whole day together. We play games in the car, tell stories, sing along to CD's, eat snacks and make every effort to enjoy each moment. We stop along the way to enjoy the scenery, or feed horses we might have seen in a field. Often we spend more time travelling in the car than we do at our destination, so it makes no sense enduring a two-hour-long journey to have just one hour of fun when you arrive! So we turn it into three hours of fun, by enjoying the entire experience.

Are you enjoying your journey or just trying to survive it? You need to get people around you who understand how to have fun and make the most boring parts of the journey enjoyable. If Paul could help Silas find joy in a prison cell, then why not get people in your world who can bring joy to even the worst parts of your journey?

I believe that we are supposed to enjoy our journey from beginning to end. 1 Timothy 6:17 says that God, *'richly provides us with everything for our enjoyment.'* At my home church we have created an atmosphere of enjoyment, which permeates everything we do. We have chosen cheerful people to be part of our staff team. Our church is filled with fun and laughter; it is a place people enjoy coming to. And Personally, I have many fun-loving friends who add enjoyment to my journey.

If you lack fun and enjoyment on your journey, then maybe you need to make some changes. Perhaps you need cheerful travelling companions to accompany you. If you spend your time with people who are not fun-loving and don't appreciate your sense of humour, then find some people who do. Jesus travelled to places where he wasn't appreciated or welcomed and he told his disciples that if they weren't welcome they should *'shake the dust off their feet'* and move on *(Matt 10:14)* Sometimes you need to have the same approach and keep travelling until you find people who love you for being you.

My travelling companions enjoy my journcy with me, and I enjoy theirs. We laugh and celebrate together along the way. There have been times when the fun friends in my life have kept me going. During difficult times I have been cushioned by the laughter and enjoyment of those around me. I believe that God wants us to enjoy our lives. So, if you aren't enjoying your journey, ask yourself why. If your journey only ever feels like hard work, then you are missing some vital travelling companions. You need to find some fun friends who will be *'good medicine'* for you along the way.

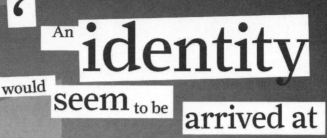

' An **identity** would seem to be arrived at by the way in which the person **faces** and **uses** his experience. '

James Baldwin

Chapter 12

The Art of Remembering

The identity journey is not an easy one to take. There are tests and trials that you must face but these are for a purpose; they are what God will use to develop the 'real you'. In fact, it is at the times when you are most under pressure that you begin to discover who you really are. David, for example, didn't know his identity was that of a giant-killer until he took on Goliath! Twelve ordinary young men didn't know their identities were that of world-changers until they journeyed with Jesus. Then there is Moses, who didn't know his true identity was that of a great leader until he set off on his journey and three million people followed him – and it is the same for you and me. We will discover the most about our true identity as we face difficult circumstances along the way.

We have to beware, though, because sometimes situations arise on the road ahead that aren't just potential set backs. There is far more to them than just another challenge to overcome. They enter your path with the intention of not just slowing you down but completely hijacking your journey.

All of us are potential candidates for a hijacking, no matter how far we have already travelled or what we have achieved. Many great people have been hijacked on the way to their destiny. Some allowed a situation to strike fear into their hearts, others stopped moving and set up camp and others just chose to settle for living someone else's life instead of pressing through on their own. Whatever the reason, they abandoned their individual journeys.

Hijackers have a strategy; they look for your point of weakness and then strike when you are most vulnerable. If you are only looking for the obvious attacks and become complacent, then you are a likely candidate for a hijacking attempt. These things are not always easy to identify and may even appear to be harmless, until it is too late. Many people fail to recognise the stealth tactics of the enemy and gradually their lives are infiltrated through the doorway of compromise.

Jacob allowed Rebekah to hijack the plan for his life at an early age; it was his complacency that made him vulnerable. The children of Israel let unbelief hijack their identity; instead of realising they were liberated to be themselves, they remained bound to their old identity as slaves and wanted to turn back from their journey. Elijah allowed his journey to be hijacked by fear and he ended up in the middle of a desert, sat under a broom tree. For Jonah it was disobedience that he allowed to infiltrate his life and he ended up in the belly of a whale. None of these people should have spent time in those places; it was not part of the route God had planned for them but they let their circumstances and a fear of what lay ahead hijack their journey.

Elijah, for example, was a man of power; an awesome prophet who had seen God do amazing miracles through his life. Yet there he sat under the broom tree, completely miserable and wanting to die, questioning his identity — something he had been so confident about before. Hijackers will force you to travel in the wrong direction and unless you learn to counter their attack, you may end up wandering in places you were never meant to go. Years of your life can be lost in just one of these detours. So, what can we do to protect against these situations, circumstances and people who can have this damaging effect on our journey?

Already in this book, we have seen the difference that having the right travelling companions can make to your journey. They can help steer you in the right direction and encourage you to keep going. There will be times however, when their input alone is not enough and their voices are silent in your world. These are the times the enemy knows you are most vulnerable and he will try to exploit the opportunity.

Remember, it was when David was alone that his journey was hijacked through the temptation of Bathsheba. Therefore, we must not build a journey that is dependent on other people being able to bale us out. If Job had done this he wouldn't have made it; he would have quit the journey by taking the bad advice of his wife who told him to, *'curse God and die,'* *(Job 2:9)*. Equally, his friends were confused by the journey he was on and the circumstances he found himself in, so they didn't have the answers he needed either. Job had to find something else to draw on. At the most challenging stage of his journey, after he had lost his health, his family and everything he owned, he had to search deep within himself to discover what direction to take. We will all experience moments like these; moments when we need more to rely on than our companions. The success of our journey is too important to let it depend solely on someone else.

The great news is that God had already equipped Job and he has already equipped you with everything you need to help you go the full distance; he is not sending you on 'mission impossible'. You just need to dig deep within yourself to find the tools he has built into your life that are able to foil every hijack attempt. This book is nearing its end, but I am only too aware that we all have a long way to go on our journeys, and for some it may just be beginning. So, before we part company and continue in the unique direction set for our individual lives, I want to look at how we can train ourselves to master the tools that will help keep us on track.

Remember, remember

The first tool is something that we all have but some of us are better at using it than others. It is a tried and tested tool that has helped many people avoid the hijack attempts made on their journey. It is the art of remembering.

Your ability to remember could be the difference between you making it or quitting in a time of testing. This tool is something that God has encouraged people to use throughout history. The words 'remember' and 'don't forget' come up again and again throughout scripture; it is something that God has emphasised for our benefit. Jesus also understood the value of remembering and often repeated important themes to help people remember his words. For example, the parables of the lost son, the lost coin and the lost sheep illustrate exactly the same point but are told three times to help the message stick in people's minds.

When we look back at Jacob's journey we can see how he also had to harness the tool of his memory in order to succeed in his journey. The path he took separated him from his family for twenty years but then came the day that he was to be reunited with Esau. Jacob was afraid because the last time they had met, Esau had threatened to kill him. I am sure that with every step he took towards their encounter he had to remind himself of the journey so far. He had to keep on recalling the words God had spoken to him and the promises over his life. He had to remember that he was no longer Jacob the deceiver but he was now Israel. I am sure his memory kept affirming in him his true identity as he reminded himself of all he had discovered. His memories from the journey gave him the courage and confidence to re-enter his brother's world.

Remembering prevents bad choices

We all have a memory but what we deliberately choose to remember will have the greatest impact on the success of our journey. Some people do not have a good memory at all; they are the people we all know who are constantly forgetting things. They have gained a reputation for having a bad memory because they turn up late for meetings they have forgotten about, can never remember where they have put their jacket, shoes or keys, and are always playing catch up because their forgetfulness slows them down. The art of remembering is a skill they have yet to perfect. But what our forgetful friends need to understand is that being forgetful in life isn't neutral. They will be labelled as unreliable, will miss out on many opportunities because they are running late and have other expenses to pay through their failure to remember. In 'hijack' moments they will suffer because they won't be able to remember the wisdom needed to find their way out of the situation.

Other people are not quite as forgetful, they have an impressive ability to remember but the problem is they have a selective memory. They tend to remember all the wrong things. So, they can easily recall the time when a friend hurt them, or the time when they tried doing something and failed, even though it was fifteen years ago! This kind of memory paralyzes you because the next time something similar happens, you remember the past and it stops you in your tracks. Some people have a frozen memory that is forever stuck on a painful event in their lives, which they are unable to move on from, so their journey gets stuck in neutral. The tool that is supposed to 'unstick' them becomes the very thing that holds them back. Instead of using it to help them go forward, it sets around their lives like cement and stops them from moving another inch in the right direction. What was supposed to be a tool to disarm the hijackers in their lives starts to have the opposite affect and de-rails their identity journey.

We need therefore to programme our memory in the right way so that it becomes useful to us. I know that on our journey as a church we have come to value and understand the power and importance of remembering. When we 'crossed over' to become the church we are today, Pastor Paul would regularly remind the church of things that happened earlier in the journey. He would remind us of how the church used to be, of things we had battled through and the new freedoms we had in the church because of it. Some people just didn't understand why he kept going over it; he even wrote a book journaling all the ups and downs of our journey. He would get letters from them saying he should stop re-living the hurt of what had happened during that time but Paul wasn't re-living it because he was unable to move on from some painful moments; he was making sure that everyone remembered what it had cost them to get this far. He was reminding them what the hijackers of 'control' and 'intimidation' looked like, so that they could easily identify them and deal with them in the future. He knew that retaining these memories would give us an internal early warning system in case these intruders ever tried to ambush our journey again. By journaling our experience in his book *Crossing Over*, he handed a gift of wisdom to any others who might travel along the same path.

Don't pay twice

My parents live in a beautiful old farm house which has some very low doorways; the front entrance door, in particular is very low. Even though the door height never changes, it's amazing how many people repeatedly bang their heads on it, even when they know it is there! They simply forget. In the same way, many people keep banging their heads against the same problems, situations and circumstances, because they can't remember the lessons they have learned previously. They end up repeating the same mistakes. They go from one relationship breakdown to another, from one bad career choice to another, from one wrong turn or dead end to another and their journey is consequently hijacked because of their poor memory. We have the power to free ourselves from this and build a different life if we become skilled at using the tool of our memory.

Storing experiences in your memory bank is like having your own internal alarm. If you don't train your memory in the right way then you are leaving an open door into your life, which any hijackers will walk straight back through. This is a frustrating and expensive way to live and you will end up paying twice for things, because the same items will be stolen from your life on more than one occasion.

In my life I have sometimes ended up paying for things twice and it has been a frustrating experience. Steve and I were on holiday in America and I had bought some expensive jeans on the last day of our trip. They were my favourite style and a brand that I couldn't buy at home in England. I handed the bag, with my prized purchase, to Steve for him to look after and asked him for it again once we reached our hotel. He couldn't remember anything about it! 'I haven't got your jeans', he said. So I described the moment I had given him the shopping bag, where we were at the time and what I had said, to try and jog his memory into action. By the time he remembered, it was too late; he had left them next to a bench in the shopping mall. I didn't get my jeans back and I had to pay out for another pair. Steve's bad memory that day meant that I had to pay twice for something that already belonged to me.

Many people have the same experience spiritually. They forget who they are in Christ, they forget what they have discovered about their identity and they forget which relationships God told them to separate from. They repeat the same mistakes and have to keep paying the same price again and again. We need to programme our memories in the right way, so that when we face the same situation we can stand up and say, 'I'm not doing this anymore, because I've already paid for that in my life and I remember what God did for me!' We need to pull out every receipt we have and wave them in the enemy's face. So, when he comes to make you pay twice, you simply pull out the receipt as you recall the price that was paid and refuse to go to war about things God has already given you victory over.

We once stayed in a hotel with a revolving door and on one occasion, my friend's young son got stuck in it on his own, going round and round. At first he thought it was funny but after a while he started to panic and quickly tired of walking round in endless circles! Some people's journeys have become like this. Although they have movement in their lives, they aren't going anywhere. They pass the same scenery by continually repeating the same mistakes. This is a frustrating place to be in but God just can't let you progress to the next stage of your journey until you learn the lessons that will help you grow and move on.

If you are someone who keeps having feelings of déjà vu in certain situations, then maybe you need to work on your memory. You need to remember what God said to you last time and use that wisdom to navigate your way through the circumstances you face, without letting them steal your momentum.

Remembering right

Our ability to not just remember but to remember the right things, is something we need to work at if we want to keep going in our identity journey.

David experienced several setbacks on his journey and he tackled them by using the tool of his memory. He called to mind all God had spoken to him and everything he had already learned. There was one particular time when he was living in the Judean desert, hiding from Saul. David was feeling vulnerable, and it would have been easy for him to let his journey be hijacked by fear or unbelief. At that moment David had many memories that he could draw upon but not all of them would have been helpful. He could have remembered that Saul wanted to kill him, he could have remembered how lonely he was feeling in the desert or the fear he felt when he had to run for his life. David didn't remember any of these; the memories he chose to lean on were the ones which would keep him moving in the right direction. He remembered God, he remembered his faithfulness, his great love and he remembered the times God had saved him from his enemies in the past. During this difficult time he wrote, *'On my bed I remember you; I think of you through the watches of the night. Because you are my help, I sing in the shadow of your wings.' (Psalm 63:6-7)*

David had learnt to use his memory in a way that helped him refocus his heart on God. It gave him the strength to sing instead of feeling sorry for himself and the courage to continue and advance with his journey.

There is so much we can learn from how David used his memories to inject fresh momentum into his journey. The Psalms are a catalogue of songs, calling to mind ammunition to help keep you moving. David had mastered the 'art of remembering' and it propelled his life forward, helping him to thwart many attempted hijackings. We also need to work at remembering what God has said to us, his awesome promises and the incredible ways he has already blessed our lives. These things are stored away in your memory bank so you can recall them when you need them most. There will be times on your journey when the only thing that will keep you going is the tool of your memory, just like Job. Despite everything that was happening he remembered God's goodness and that was enough for him to keep going.

The Art of Remembering

We each have an individual responsibility to work on improving our ability to remember because it is such a vital piece of equipment for the journey. No matter what your journey brings, you have to know his truth for yourself. You need to remember that God is your healer, because when sickness comes, sometimes it is all you have to stand on — so pull out that receipt and stand on it! You need to remember that God is your provider and the lover of your soul if you want to be able to walk through times of trial without faltering in your steps. The power of remembering will help you keep your momentum no matter what twists and turns your journey holds.

So, become skilled in using the tool of your memory if you want to keep going for the long haul. Once you become skilled at memorising these valuable lessons from your past, you will discover a new momentum for your journey that will 'fast forward' you into the future God has planned for you. Train your memory to work to your advantage. It will remind you of all that God has done in your life and of the future he has promised you. This will give you the inner strength and resolve to resist any future hijack attempts.

Chapter 13

Flint Face

Many people set off enthusiastically on their identity journey but then get distracted and never achieve what they had hoped for. Instead of being one hundred percent committed to their journey, they procrastinate, put their ideas on the back burner and start dawdling. Distractions are expert at hijacking your journey without you even realising what is happening. What started as a sprint can become a wander; what started with purpose and speed can become a meander and what started with great determination can become a dawdle. Often people start well and with great enthusiasm, claiming they want to do amazing things with their lives but when it is time to get moving they stand still. They don't have the perseverance to make their dreams a reality, and are easily distracted from their purpose by the busyness of life.

You will only get the most out of your journey if you are completely determined. There has to be something inside you that will not give in. You need to find a steely resolve that will make you roll up your sleeves and get on with it. This determination is a tool that God has put in your life to help you push through. It is something every adventurous traveller needs to carry with them because it will cut through excuses, distractions and any other obstacle in your path. It will take you past the point of no return on your journey so that there is simply no going back! You need to get some of this flint-like determination in your life.

Flint is an incredibly strong stone. It is not pliable, does not crumble or crack under pressure, it is hard and strong. It can be used as a tool to cut through strong materials and can also be used to sharpen blunt instruments. This stone represents an attitude and a resilience that we all need to have — one which God gave Ezekiel for his journey.

Ezekiel needed a great measure of determination if he was to succeed on his journey. He needed to be so convinced and determined that he could break through any resistance he faced. He had been given the difficult job of confronting the people of Israel about their sin and its consequences — something they didn't want to hear about — so he needed to be forceful enough to break through any resistance or opposition.

God spoke into Ezekiel's situation saying, *'But the house of Israel is not willing to listen to you because they are not willing to listen to me, for the whole house of Israel is hardened and obstinate. But I will make you as unyielding and hardened as they are. I will*

make your forehead like the hardest stone, harder than flint.'
(Ezekiel 3:7-9)

God told Ezekiel that having a 'flint-face' would give him the hard, unbreakable edge he needed to make his journey a success. This is something you also need to help you on your way. There are some things you are supposed to do and some places you need to pass through. Whether or not you get there will depend on whether or not you have learned how to get this quality into your life and 'set your face like flint'.

Set your plans

This book has thrown up many questions and possibilities. It has asked you to consider what you are aiming for in life and what you hope to achieve on your journey. Are you being true to the real you? Whose life are you leading? What are you going to separate from, and who are you planning to connect your life to? Unless you have a flint-face your chances of making real progress and moving towards those desires is limited.

In order to 'set your face like flint' you have to make a commitment and resolve to stay true to who you are. You have to take a non-negotiable decision to never turn back. This will help you move beyond any circumstances that may try to stop you from progressing. Jacob needed this kind of determination when he knew he had to leave Laban. He was offered a tempting pay-rise in an attempt to persuade him to stay. It didn't work because Jacob had decided where he was going on his journey and had a flint-like commitment to keep moving towards it.

In the Garden of Eden, Adam was not flint-faced about what God had said about his journey. Eve opened up the non-negotiable subject of the 'tree of the knowledge of good and evil' for discussion. If the unbending quality of flint had been in Adam's life, then his journey and the journey of all who travelled after him, would have been very different.

Your determination to keep travelling in the right direction also needs to be like this. If you choose to relax, to compromise and make excuses for the lack of momentum in your life, suddenly you will realise that another year has gone by. You will have missed out on those God-given opportunities, that relationship or friendship that could have been such a blessing to your life, if only you had pursued it. I don't want your life to be full of regrets about times when you should have moved forward but didn't, because you couldn't stand firm.

Wherever you are on your identity journey, you need to set your face like flint. You need to make some decisions about what you want to achieve spiritually and naturally, and get to work. If you learn to do this it will give you the determination you need to turn your plans and dreams into reality.

Set your scales

In Deuteronomy we read: *'Do not have two differing weights in your bag — one heavy, one light. Do not have two differing measures in your house — one large, one small. You must have accurate and honest weights and measures, so that you may live long in the land the Lord your God is giving you. For the Lord your God detests anyone who does these things, anyone who deals dishonestly.' (25:13-16)*

This scripture is talking about the way business people conducted their transactions at that time. They carried weights with them, so if someone wanted to buy a pound of food or grain, they would have a stone to represent that weight. Some people had differing sizes of rocks that weren't accurate — they were being dishonest and cheating one another, depending on who was buying the goods from them.

It is possible to have differing weights and measures in your life that don't match up to the standards God has set. His standards are non-negotiable, because he put them in place to safeguard your journey. You need to have a flint-faced attitude to them, because they are there to help you maintain your momentum. No area of our lives should operate with a differing weight and measure, but sometimes our standards can be more like jelly than flint. Jelly is not a substance that copes well under pressure! It starts to wobble with only the slightest bit of force exerted on it and that is how shaky some people can be; their standards are pliable, changeable and they have one rule for one person and a different rule for another.

Proverbs 20:10 says, '*God detests differing weights and hates dishonest scales.*' I think we should pay attention to anything that God detests and make sure we are not guilty of doing something that is so against the nature and heart of God. We need to have a flint-faced approach to the standards we use on our journey in church, business, family life and our relational world. Even when our weights and measures are just slightly out and we think we can get away with it, beware, because any lack of accuracy will be detrimental to our progress and can hijack our journey.

People pleasers

There are many different factors that can knock our weights and scales off balance. For myself, I discovered early on in my journey, that people had the potential to affect my scales.

When I was first in ministry, there was a particular person who used to really intimidate me. It seemed they constantly undermined and criticised me. Every time I spoke, they would question what I was saying and try to silence my voice. I soon began to realise that their presence was beginning to affect me. So, if this person was around on the day I was due to preach, I would subconsciously water down my message. I'd say, 'I think God might be saying,' instead of, 'I know God is saying' and I didn't speak from the conviction of my heart. I was allowing their attitude to make me question my own identity and it stopped me from expressing the 'real me' whenever they were around. God challenged me about this compromise and I realised that my identity journey was grinding to a halt, because I was becoming a leader whose weights and measures changed depending on how people responded to me. Saul was like that and he lost everything because of it. When God took his hand off him, Saul admitted that he had become a people pleaser (1 Samuel 15:24). We simply cannot afford to let people change our God-chosen direction.

We need to examine our lives and ask what kind of people affect our weights and measures? Is it people you feel intimidated by, is it people that you struggle to love, or even your family? We read earlier in this book how David let himself be blinded by a family tie to his son Absalom and it nearly hijacked his journey. Too many times I have seen people judge others harshly and then turn a blind eye to the same form of compromise in their close family and friends. This type of differing weights and measures will hurt you and be a stumbling block on the journey ahead. It makes no difference who you have changed your scales for, or the reason why.

You need to set your face like flint, get rid of your faulty standards and become consistent and steadfast in the way you set your scales.

Lessons from a leper

There is an amazing story in 2 Kings chapter 7 about four lepers. These men had been treated as outcasts for their entire lives. Their journey had been long and difficult and they had been labelled with the unwanted badge of 'leper'. As far as the people in the city were concerned, that was their identity; their leprosy was what would define them for the rest of their lives. The stigma that went with the label meant they were thrown out of the city and separated from their families, because of their disease. At that time there was a famine in their home city as a result of an enemy siege. People were starving to death. It got so bad, that as a last resort, they were boiling their babies and eating bird poo; they were completely desperate!

The lepers reasoned that if they stayed near their home city they would die and if they left, they would be killed by their enemies. So, having nothing to lose but knowing the enemy had food, they decided to approach the enemy and see if they would live or die. They arrived to find an empty camp with comfortable beds and warm shelter. The enemy had fled, leaving behind all their food and provisions. These four guys, who had been so badly treated by their own community and given a different measure of grace, love and dignity to other city inhabitants, now had plenty. What would you have done? I think I would have said, 'It serves them right, God has blessed us and now it is their turn to suffer!' But what happened next was amazing. As they sat down to eat, one of the lepers said, 'It's not right that we sit down and enjoy this, we need to tell the people in the city that there is food here because they are starving to death.'

The leper had a set weight and measure in his life and he would not allow his circumstances, or the way he had been treated, to alter it. He refused to do to others what had been done to him. He responded with an opposite spirit and showed that his true identity was different to the one he had been given. He knew what it was like to be excluded and was determined to live with a greater measure of love and inclusion, even though the people in the city had been his tormentors. His largeness of heart broke the ongoing cycle of inconsistency and many lives were saved that day. We can learn so much from the life of this man.

Don't let the way you have been treated affect your weights and measures. Don't let hurts live again through injustice to others. Determine the scales for your life now. Set the weights and leave them alone.

Sidetrack situations

Often, adversity can tip the scales of your life. At times like this the real 'you' is exposed, because when things are going well, it is easy to put on a show and look good but circumstances expose what is really happening below the surface.

It's easy for someone to look like they are full of peace, until the storm hits; that's when you see them panic! This pattern is often easy to spot in church. If life is going well, some Christians are full of enthusiasm; they sit at the front of church and worship God with every ounce of their energy and passion. Just a week later though, the same person can be sitting on the back row, looking miserable and hardly singing a word when the band starts to play. The only difference is that their circumstances have changed. Maybe they have been made redundant or maybe they have simply had a row with their husband or wife on the way to church. People can be so inconsistent and can let their circumstances affect the measure they use towards God. One week they would go to the ends of the earth for him and the next they let their faith take a nosedive, because something didn't turn out as they had hoped. This behaviour is what God detests; it is differing weights and measures of commitment and gratitude; measures that are not set like flint but are altered by circumstances.

This inconsistency will derail your journey time after time. The truth is, circumstances will come and go but your determination and momentum doesn't have to.

Having a flint-faced determination in our lives will make us tough enough to withstand whatever circumstances we encounter on our way, without crumbling or giving way.

The problem for many travellers is that our feelings get in the way of our journey. How we feel can be such a dominant factor in how well we do. We need to bring our feelings into line and straighten them out, using God's word. No one is immune from feelings and the truth is, some days you will not 'feel' like travelling any further. Our feelings can be like a speedometer on our journey. When we feel good about life, it's all systems go and we set off at a breakneck pace but when the going gets tough, we slam the brakes on and start crawling along, because we just don't 'feel' like going anywhere! We need to learn how to manage our feelings, otherwise our journey will continually stop and start. Feelings are expert in the art of hijacking; they will lie to you, rob you and leave you contemplating destinations that were never supposed to be on your itinerary. If you don't believe me, then just look at Jonah. His feelings got him inside of a whale!

It's not just your own feelings that you need to keep in check along your journey. Some people don't just allow their emotions to cause inconsistency in their own lives, also they use them to try and manipulate others. Feelings can be very persuasive and we need to control their power.

Before speed cameras arrived, I never had a ticket. I was immune from them, because I could trade on my feelings. I remember one occasion when I had been having an awful day. Steve and I had just moved into a new house and we had been busy sorting everything out. I nipped out to the shop nearby to get some paint. I was in a hurry and didn't even notice the police car that had followed my speeding car home, until it parked behind me on my drive! I explained to the policeman how sorry I was. I told him how everything had gone wrong and I began to cry to let him know how I felt about the situation. In the end he didn't give me a ticket, he was just glad to escape this mad, emotional woman! My feelings manipulated his decision that day.

However, speed cameras are different. The ticket just arrives through your door with three points on your driving licence and a £60 fine. You can't talk to it and explain why you don't deserve it, because feelings have been eliminated from the equation. They don't feel sorry for you and you can't reason with them. They have a set weight and measure for every person that drives past them above the speed limit. Many Christians and even some entire churches, need to fit spiritual speed cameras that show all who enter their sphere that this is a zone with a set way of operating. It sends a message to all other travellers who they may encounter the standards that have been set. It makes it clear that they are not open to emotional manipulation from 'Rebekah's', neither will they be held back by 'Laban's' control, or react like 'Esau' expects them to.

This is something you must set your face like flint about. Refuse to live your journey constantly being manipulated by your feelings or the feelings of others. How you feel is really irrelevant, if you know what you should do. God expects us to rise above our feelings and get on with our journey. Imagine if Jesus had let his feelings determine whether or not he went to the cross. It was obvious that he was in agony about the journey he had to take; he cried out to the Father to see if the burden could be lifted from him. However, his words, *'Yet not my will, but yours be done' (Luke 22:42)*, were the language of flint. It showed determination to continue on the journey and bypass feelings. If Jesus hadn't done this, we wouldn't have been set free to go on our journey. So, in order to make it all worthwhile, we must not settle for anything less.

One of the challenges facing us today as God's people is staying consistent in an ever-changing society. We live in a time and culture where people constantly change their minds but we need to have a flint-faced determination to live differently. Your life is supposed to be a race and one that you must be determined to win. It says in 1 Corinthians 9:24, *'Do you not know that in a race all the runners run, but only one gets the prize? Run in such a way as to get a prize.'*

If you try to run with differing weights and measures, they will trip you up; if you want to win you cannot let other people slow you down by their emotional manipulation. There are some things in life that you simply must be flint-faced about. Be determined, make plans and set your scales in every area of your life. This will bring a new level of consistency to your walk, it will protect your life from being hijacked and help you build the kind of life that God can use. If you are going to run, then you might as well run to win!

Chapter 14

Living a Stand Out Life

Some people always stand out from the crowd. It's hard to work out why; they just do life differently. They are unafraid to express who they are, they will stand up for what they believe no matter what other people think of them and keep travelling. Their journey has momentum, they are focused on their destination and busy doing all God has called them to do. You can't hijack their journey and they won't slow down long enough to pick up unwanted hitchhikers from the side of the road, who may try to persuade them to take a detour.

Every year thousands of people compete in the London Marathon. It always attracts massive press coverage and I am often amazed what some people will do to make themselves stand out. They will dress in the most ridiculous outfits and come up with eye-catching gimmicks to set them apart from everyone else. In the race you are called to run, your identity journey, being the 'real you' will make you stand out from all other runners. Being the unique individual you were created to be, will give you a distinctive life.

Throughout history there have always been people whose lives and journeys have stood out from the crowd. But why, out of the millions of people God created, did certain individuals attract his attention so much that he chose to use their lives in an amazing way? The Bible is a book full of stories about people who stood out from the crowd. They didn't allow their journeys to be hijacked by the status quo or the agenda of others. They didn't waste time by allowing others, who would take them off track, to board their lives. They lived life getting out who they really were and because of that, their journeys are recorded for ever.

It makes me think about people like Noah. Out of all the people on the earth why did God choose him to build the Ark? What was it about a shepherd boy called David that made him a suitable candidate to be King? What did God see in the lives of people like Abraham, Moses, Joshua, Elijah and Jeremiah that made him design a purpose for their lives way beyond what anyone would consider normal? One factor was their determination to stay true to who they were and to go against the flow.

Caleb became one of those outstanding lives. His journey was recorded but when you read about it, you cannot escape the point that he was just one of three million others who had exactly the same opportunity to stand out. Caleb was one of the twelve spies sent into Canaan but do you recognise the names Shaphat, Igal,

Palti, Ammiel, Sethur and Nahbi? These were some of the other men who went on the same reconnaissance mission into Canaan but their lives didn't stand out. They all had the same badge of 'leader' as Caleb but the label they wore did not reflect who they really were. These so called 'leaders' did not have what was required to do the job. Caleb's true identity was that of a great leader and this meant he couldn't help but take on all opposition and do what he believed was right. That made his life very useful to God and this is why we remember Caleb's journey. It wasn't because he was related to the rich and famous, it wasn't because he was pushy and wanted recognition, nor was it because he was seen in the right places. Caleb stood out because he knew who he was; he had set the co-ordinates for his journey and this set him apart from the crowd.

When the spies returned from their trip, they described the incredible land they had travelled through. They told the people how rich it was, that it had an abundance of luscious fruit and fertile soil. But they also brought a bad report explaining that there were giants in the land and there was simply no way they could take it for their own. Their feelings of insecurity and weakness hijacked the journey they were supposed to embark upon. It says in Numbers 13:30, *'Then Caleb silenced the people before Moses and said, "We should go up and take possession of the land, for we can certainly do it."'*

Caleb stood out, he was not prepared to blend in and his behaviour was opposite to the accepted norm. He went against what had been said, silenced the people and spoke from his convictions. Caleb was not prepared to go along with them for the sake of a quiet life. He stayed true to who he was and what he believed in.

The other spies went with the majority consensus. This was a decision based on who they thought they were; they had an identity crisis because they saw themselves as small and the enemy as large. Caleb saw himself differently; his identity was that of a leader. He knew he was one of God's children and this is why he was convinced their mission to take the land could not fail. The other spies didn't have the conviction of Caleb, or enough faith in God's promises to keep moving forward. The bad report they gave was fair and realistic as far as they were concerned, compared to the outlandish claims of Caleb and his 'stand out' friend, Joshua.

We need to recognise that people of a normal spirit can often sound very reasonable. Sometimes their arguments can make a lot of sense and that is why they manage to influence the opinions of others. They refuse to be unique or to stand out by journeying alone if necessary; they will not separate from the norm or remove the 'stabiliser' of safety in numbers. The other spies didn't want to risk being labelled as mavericks like Caleb but often this is how others see you if your life stands out.

Normal living may give you a comfortable life but it will not take you on a journey of adventure and discovery. It is something that will make your life indistinguishable from others who have also chosen to live life at a level called average. If you want your journey to be one that attracts the attention of heaven, you must live a distinctive life. As God's people and his House we are called to be a vibrant expression of his life on the earth and for this to happen, we must stand out!

Distinctive living

If you decide to embark upon your identity journey, then your life will have certain stand out qualities to it. As we have already seen throughout this book, your journey settles issues in your life about who you are and the direction you must take. This instills a new level of conviction in your heart to keep going and a flint-like determination to succeed.

The name Caleb actually means 'snappish dog' and that is a great picture of what a person with conviction looks like. A dog that wants to bite that postman has a steely determination that will not let him give up until he sinks his teeth in! Caleb was a man of conviction like his name suggested. Caleb lived among three million moaning, whining people but refused to let go of the deep conviction he held that the promised land belonged to them. People of conviction see the possibilities not the problems and when Caleb went to spy out the land, to him it was a done deal. He thought he was just taking a look around his new home but the other spies, except for Joshua, were terrified by what they saw. Caleb's conviction gave him a different perspective to his companions.

People of conviction are like this. They will not back down or change their route to keep other people happy; nor will they be persuaded to down-scale their dreams. On your journey, you need to get to a place where you are completely convinced about the path you are on. Your convictions will take you past the negative report and perspective that others have of the situation. They will keep you travelling in the right direction when those around you are being knocked off course by the same circumstances. Conviction is a driving force which adds momentum to your journey, it keeps you focused and makes it difficult for you to be distracted.

As you continue on your journey, the amount of conviction in your heart will grow with each step you take. It will give you the push you need to separate from 'Rebekah'; it will make you determined to wrestle with God to find the answers to your questions. Conviction will compel you to say what needs to be said and challenge the people you need to confront. It will take the brakes off your life and journey, by freeing you to express who you really are, and do what you were born to do.

Being a person of conviction can be a lonely road to travel, at times, because standing out is not always a comfortable experience. By going against the flow, you leave yourself wide open for criticism from those who have decided to travel with the crowd. People who prefer to blend in rather than stand out, will not appreciate you disturbing their peace with your enthusiasm and challenging words. They will want you to shut up, calm down and stop getting so carried away.

This is what happened to Caleb and Joshua that day. They were the only ones out of the twelve spies who urged the people to take the land. They appealed to the people and expressed their resolute belief that it was their rightful inheritance. God himself had promised it to them! In Numbers 14, we can see what happened. *'Joshua son of Nun and Caleb son of Jephunneh, who were among those who had explored the land, tore their clothes and said to the entire Israelite assembly, "The land we passed through and explored is exceedingly good,"' (Numbers 14:6-7).* Tearing their clothes was unusual behaviour but having a stand-out spirit will often cause you to act in a way that makes your journey unique. Sometimes you will do things that look crazy to those around you, in order to stay true to your journey.

The forceful stand they took didn't have the desired effect; they did manage to stir up the people but not in the way they had hoped. The people of Israel started grumbling against Moses and Aaron yet again and even dared to suggest that they would be better off back in Egypt. Caleb and Joshua could not walk away without expressing the deep convictions that were burning in their hearts. They kept appealing to the people saying, *'Do not be afraid of the people of the land, because we will swallow them up. Their protection is gone, but the Lord is with us. Do not be afraid of them. But the whole assembly talked about stoning them.'(Numbers 14:9-10)*

You need to be able to handle the fact that some people may want to throw a stone in your direction to knock you down if they don't like what you're saying. If you want to live as a person of conviction you will face similar experiences.

I remember when I went to University. The environment and atmosphere could be very hostile towards anyone who went against the norm of what was politically correct. That atmosphere can make you fearful of speaking up, because you know that standing out may cause others to alienate you. But Caleb didn't even consider that, he had decided that he would rather be in trouble with people than God, so he kept going.

Put your whole self in

Finally, of Caleb we read: *'But because my servant Caleb has a different spirit and follows me wholeheartedly, I will bring him into the land he went to, and his descendants will inherit it.'* (*Numbers 14:24*)

Caleb inherited the promised land, he reached his destination but three million people who set out on the same journey died in the desert. Their inheritance was the same; they shared the same promise and walked the same road but were hijacked on the way by complacency, unbelief and disobedience. A promise that was meant for generations of people, one that they all had the credentials to claim, went to one man called Caleb.

Sometimes we can see incredible blessing poured out on the life of someone like Caleb and think that they have been singled out as one of God's favourites. Yet each one of the Children of Israel could have entered the land, it wasn't an issue of favouritism. The only difference between them was that Caleb believed God's promises and they didn't.

Wholehearted people do not quit; they have an energy and zest for life that keeps them going. If you are wholehearted you will not question your direction, you will not question the discoveries you have made about your identity and purpose in life, even on your worst and most difficult days. Continuing on your identity journey will make you move from half-hearted to wholehearted living. You may think you are whole hearted now but you will discover a greater measure when you commit to being everything God has called you to be.

When I first thought of launching our women's conference, Cherish, I received a very half-hearted response from a small group of women. They said that people wouldn't want to come to a women's ministry event and that it would be a disaster. My wholehearted conviction was what eventually overwhelmed them and helped to change and influence their opinion. Today, thousands of women have been blessed but it wasn't my own skills or abilities that made it possible; it was my wholehearted determination.

A half-hearted approach to your journey is the equivalent of trying to drive with your handbrake on. It will be a form of resistance to your forward movement; it makes progress a far more difficult prospect than it should be. Half-heartedness is a tiring way to live, which eventually will wear you out, cause you to stop and put your journey on hold.

Are you living a wholehearted life today? Are you wholehearted about your life, about your family, your marriage, your church and about continuing with your journey? Wholehearted living will make you stand out.

Go the distance

I really want you to make it on your journey. My heart is that your journey will be one worth remembering, that you will make your own unique mark on the world and on the lives of the people around you. This journey is not a short trip; to complete it means having the dedication and commitment to keep moving. It means you must keep challenging yourself to grow, change and become the person God created you to be, day after day, year after year. It takes stamina and determination to journey this way. It took Caleb forty- five years to reach his chosen destination of the promised land. He had watched vast numbers of people perish in the desert because of their unbelief but that had still not deterred him from his deep conviction that he would get there. I love the passage in Joshua that describes what happened when Caleb finally received his inheritance.

When Joshua was dividing up the land Caleb said, *'So here I am today, eighty-five years old! I am still as strong today as the day Moses sent me out; I'm just as vigorous to go out to battle now as I was then. Now give me this hill country that the Lord promised me that day.' (Joshua 14:10-12a)*

You may think that by then, Caleb would have been satisfied with his achievements, that he would have looked back on his long journey and decided that he had reached the end of his travels but Caleb had not let anything dampen his appetite for life. This man, at the grand old age of eighty-five, still had momentum; he was still travelling. Even reaching the promised land did not make him want to put his feet up and rest. He still wanted to go further, he wanted to keep going, to keep growing his life, to dream bigger and achieve more. This level of stamina is a hallmark of having a stand-out life. It's not of your own making but from God and it keeps you going. People who stand out never stop travelling; their journey never ends. That is the kind of journey that I want to live, always stretching myself and extending the size of my life and dreams.

Stand out journeys

Certain journeys are remembered, they are noted down in history as milestones and a mark of progress and achievement. Most people have heard about the first voyage to the moon, they know who was the first to climb Mount Everest and which intrepid explorer discovered the New World. It was the uniqueness of these journeys that made them special. These people did not live within the realms of what others thought was normal or possible and this gave their lives a distinctive and memorable quality. They had the conviction and belief to follow what was in their hearts and realise the potential that was in their lives. They were immovable from the course they were determined to follow; and this caused their journeys to stand out.

I don't believe that any of these people woke up one day and decided to complete one of these amazing feats; it started with a desire and it started with a dream that compelled them to take a step. I am sure that others tried to take the same route but turned back when the road was steep; they weren't willing to pay the price it would take to reach their destination. They lacked the conviction they needed to keep them going, or chose the wrong companions for their trip. Others didn't make it because they allowed their attempt to be hijacked by criticism, by complacency or by unbelief. So, what separated out those who succeeded from those who failed? It was their willingness to put one foot in front of the other and start moving in the right direction, it was their courage to express who they were and boldly reveal their true identities to those around as they kept travelling.

Every great and memorable journey starts the same way, every mountain is climbed step by step and every marathon is run mile by mile. So I want to encourage you to keep moving, no matter how far you have already travelled or how far you still have to go. Your life is special, you are original and unique in every way and God has a journey for you to take. It is one that he has equipped you for and it is one that will also lead you to a land of discovery and adventure. This journey will cause you to discover who you really are; it will cause you to travel past the permissions of other people and beyond any labels or badges that your life has been defined by. It will connect you to new travelling companions who have the enthusiasm and experience to accompany you on your way. Every step you take will bring you closer to answering the question God wants to ask you; it is the same question that he asked of Jacob, of Gideon, of David and of every person who has lived a life that made a mark on history. He wants you to discover your true identity and to live your life expressing that to the full, one hundred percent. He wants to ask, "What is your name?"

This book has itself been a journey about identity, it has been one which has aimed to help you examine the very heart of what makes you unique. I hope it has helped you re-evaluate your life, your relationships and the direction you need to travel, if you are to live your life how God intended, expressing the real you.

Writing this book has made me so aware of the thousands of Christians who have chosen to blend in with the crowd. They are, for the most part, faceless and nameless and their journeys have been hijacked by other people's agendas, wrong labels and roles. If you identify with them, I have written this book for you. My prayer is that it will give you some new tools to help you start out on your own unique path; that it will give you the encouragement you need to break out from living a 'normal' life and to journey forward. The world needs you to be all God intended you to be; the most precious gift you can give is to be the 'real you'. I pray that you will find the courage to stand up and that by doing so, you will soon stand out.

I am also writing this book for all those whose journey has come to a standstill. They have been hijacked by 'Rebekah' and have believed the lie that their true identity was not worth pursuing. If that is you today, I want you to know beyond doubt that your future depends on you breaking free. The conviction you need to start moving towards your destiny again awaits you at the other side of the wrestle God is taking you into. Be courageous and be determined in making the right choices for your life, which will kick-start your momentum. All along, you have believed you were 'Jacob' and you have lived someone else's life but now it's time for you to become 'Israel'. You need to wrestle with God to find out who you really are and it's never too late to start.

The final group of people I am writing this book for have already travelled a long distance on their journey. They left 'Rebekah' long ago, they wrestled with God to discover their identity and are now limping in the direction of their dreams, living a stand-out life. If this describes you, then I want to urge you to keep going, because your identity journey is for the long haul. Many great travellers before you have started well but were knocked off course. You need to keep moving in the right direction, staying in step with God for your entire life. I want to encourage you to follow Caleb's example because he was still full of energy and vigour for his journey until the very end and retirement was never an option for his life. There is always more to discover about the 'real you', there are new battles to fight and more ground to take. There are also many people who need your journeying wisdom, so that together you can discover the reason you were put on the planet. You can celebrate your uniqueness, enjoy your journey and experience the deep fulfilment that only comes when you live being one hundred percent you.

So, fellow traveller, wherever this journey finds you today, I pray that you will enjoy your own path, appreciate your travelling companions and make your life stand out. Stay strong and stay true to who you are. Remember that excitement, adventure and fulfilment await you. It's all in the journey.

'Success means having the courage, the determination, and the will to become the person you believe you were meant to be.'

George Sheehan

Thank you

Thank you to all my travelling friends near and far. I am so glad we are journeying together.

Thank you for sharing my journey. Your laughter has made the hard parts easier and your companionship has turned trials into triumphs.

Thank you for the joy you bring to my world, for the encouragement to my soul and the guiding wisdom to my steps. You amaze me and I am forever indebted to you all.

Here's to the rest of the adventure!

Love ya!
Charl

Identity

By the same Author:

Consumer or Consumed?

David wrote, 'Zeal for your House consumes me.' So what about you?

In every House there are two types of people, consumers and the consumed. Over the years, God's House has been given a bad reputation because it has served the consumers of church life and marginalized those with a genuine zeal.

In this challenging and insightful book, Charlotte takes a look 'through the keyhole' to explore just what we should be seeing and hearing in God's House, and shares practical wisdom to equip everyone involved in building the church today.

This book includes a specially created DVD with video tracks demonstrating the consumed heart of the Abundant Life Church.

Identity

By the same Author:

In Her Shoes

Have you ever wondered what life would be like if you exchanged shoes with the broken and the hurting, or the lost and the orphaned? That is exactly what Jesus did and now God is looking for those who are willing to follow his example, to step out of their own comfortable shoes and walk in the shoes of another. By swapping shoes with others we deepen our empathy, increase our compassion and enlarge our world.

Whose shoes can you step into today?

Further Resources:

For more information about teaching resources of Charlotte Gambill and conferences hosted by Charlotte please visit our online store at www.alm.org.uk/shop or visit www.charlottegambill.com

Abundant Life Church
Wapping Road, Bradford
West Yorkshire
BD3 OEQ
Tel: +44 (0) 1274 307233
Email: admin@alm.org.uk
www.alm.org.uk

CHERISH FOUNDATION

This ministry is very special to me. I started it after hearing God whisper to my heart several years ago and tell me to do something to honour and place value to those who feel they are not valued. To celebrate those who have never felt celebrated and to step into the shoes of the victim, the betrayed, the abused and create a place where they can see just how loved they are. A place where we let them know they are not alone and rally an army of women to cheer them on.

Each year at our Cherish women's conference we devote an evening to do just that. We tell the story of how different ones have walked through trials and survived, and them we present them with amazing gifts to say "We believe in you.' From cars to once in a lifetime holidays we give something that will bless their world. For many it's the first time they have experienced that kind of generosity and sense of value. The foundation is made possible by the generosity of women who give each year to this great cause.

For more information and to find out how you can attend on these evenings visit: www.alm.org.uk/cherish